The
Elven
Cookbook

Thunder Bay Press
An imprint of Printers Row Publishing Group
9717 Pacific Heights Blvd, San Diego, CA 92121
www.thunderbaybooks.com • mail@thunderbaybooks.com

Printers Row Publishing Group is a division of Readerlink Distribution Services, LLC.
Thunder Bay Press is a registered trademark of Readerlink Distribution Services, LLC.

Correspondence regarding the content of this book should be sent to Thunder Bay
Press, Editorial Department, at the above address. Author and rights inquiries should be
addressed to Pyramid, an imprint of Octopus Publishing Group Ltd., Carmelite House,
50 Victoria Embankment, London, EC4Y 0DZ
www.octopusbooks.co.uk

Thunder Bay Press
Publisher: Peter Norton • Associate Publisher: Ana Parker
Editor: Dan Mansfield

Produced by Pyramid
Publisher: Lucy Pessell
Editor: Sarah Kennedy • Designer: Hannah Coughlin
Editorial Assistant: Emily Martin
Recipe Development: Jane Birch
Production Controllers: Nic Jones and Lucy Carter

Library of Congress Control Number: 2022934673

ISBN: 978-1-6672-0237-2

Printed in China

26 25 24 23 22 1 2 3 4 5

The
Elven
Cookbook

Recipes Inspired by
the Elves of Tolkien

Robert Tuesley Anderson

Thunder Bay
P·R·E·S·S

San Diego, California

Contents

Introduction

We know far less about Tolkien's Elves' eating traditions, customs, and meals than his Hobbits' or Men's—there is certainly nothing to compare, in all our encounters with this immortal, otherworldly people, with the blow-by-blow account of the "unexpected" tea party we are treated to at the start of *The Hobbit*. We do not know how many meals the Elves ate in a day—though we imagine certainly not the five the food-oriented Hobbits aspire to—nor do we get to know what their favorite ingredients or dishes are. Generally, Tolkien keeps his readers' prying eyes away from the Elves' domestic lives, and thereby points up their difference from the other, "earthier" peoples of Middle-earth. The Elves may be a part of the world, but they somehow live in a different atmosphere.

What is certain is that the Elves do eat and drink, and appear to enjoy doing so. Immortal they may be, but they are subject to hunger, as the Exiles' epic trek across the Grinding Ice in *The Silmarillion* reveals. And they are fond of feasting and merrymaking—there are frequent references to feasts of welcome and celebration in the tales of Beleriand—and from *The Hobbit* we know that the Elvenking of Mirkwood (Thranduil) is more than partial to good red wine, imported in large numbers of barrels from the East. Thranduil, it seems, is as greedy as any Dwarf or Hobbit, and his example, along with those of several other Elves, suggests that they may not be quite as ethereal and appetite-less as they might at first appear. The tantalizing glimpse—or should we say smell?—of the roasting meatballs and baking bannocks that Bilbo encounters when he first arrives in Rivendell during the Quest of Erebor certainly suggests a more complex picture of Elvish cuisine than the fresh draughts, gathered fruits and vegetables, and sustaining waybreads that otherwise seem to predominate. Elves are certainly not (at least not solely) vegan ascetics.

In both *The Lord of the Rings* and *The Hobbit*, we often feel we are sitting down to dine with the adventurers—tucking into a bowl of buttered mushrooms at Farmer Maggot's kitchen table, cutting into a fragrant blackberry tart at the Prancing Pony in Bree or spooning cream and honey onto bread in the house of Tom Bombadil. We become Frodo, Sam, Merry, and Pippin's table companions, all the while drawing on our own memories of food to enhance our enjoyment, our savoring, of Tolkien's consummate storytelling.

The Elven Cookbook

This is not the case with the Elves—it is hard to imagine sharing a dish of rabbit stew with Lady Galadriel—so one of the primary goals of the following collection of recipes is to fill that gap: to let us dine and make merry with the Elves.

The Eldar—to give the Elves their true name—are by no means a monolithic people—in their characteristics, their languages, and their cultures, they are if anything more various than Men (see the diagram on page 9). Tolkien devoted volumes to imagining and developing the Elvish kindreds and their histories—stretching back into the deepest past—and created the vast diversity of landscapes in which they lived—forest, mountain, valleys, sea coast—and the flora and fauna that flourished alongside them. It is to these exhaustive details that we must look if we want more clues about what the Elves ate and drank.

For example, of all Tolkien's kindreds of Elves, the group known as the Teleri are the most closely associated with the sea and seafaring. The evolution of the various kindreds, as described in *The Silmarillion*, are extremely complex: originally the Teleri were the third and most numerous of the houses of the Eldar (Firstborn) that awoke in the far east of Middle-earth and were led by two brothers, Elwë and Olwë. Even in this kindred's earliest days, Tolkien tells us, they began to build rafts, then boats, and finally ships to sail on the great inland Sea of Rhûn, so we can imagine that, even at this 'prehistory," they loved to cook the fish that lived in this vast freshwater lake, and the rivers and streams that flowed into it. Tolkien subsequently shows how the Teleri's love of Middle-earth's waters grows still deeper when they reach the shores of Beleriand, where they also find a protector in the Maia Ossë, a spirit of the seas. The Vala Ulmo—Tolkien's Poseidon or Neptune of a kind— arrives to take the Teleri across the ocean to Valinor, tethering an island to the shore to act as a ferry and then anchoring the island ferry far out at sea. On

this island, Tol Eressëa, the Teleri—now known as the Sea-Elves—live for many years, until, aided by Ossë, they build ships and migrate westward to Aman, settling on its shores next to their beloved sea. The Teleri must have been expert fishermen as well as shipbuilders, although Tolkien is silent on this matter. We can well imagine the Teleri swan-ships bringing home vast catches of fish, lobsters, and other seafoods to the port city of Alqualondë, to feed the kindred's burgeoning population, as well as the gathering of seaweeds, mussels, and other fruits of the shores and inlets as they sought to add still further variety and interest to the Teleri's pescatarian cuisine.

So while this book is arranged much as many a traditional cookbook— with sections on breakfast, light meals, main courses, desserts, and drinks, with an additional section on feasting and sharing—there is constant reference to the kindreds of Elves and their characteristics, so in association with the seafaring Teleri, for example, you will find plenty of fish and seafood dishes while for the woodland-loving Sindarin, you'll find an array of delicious recipes focused on game, nuts, and berries.

Kindred by kindred, landscape by landscape, the book aims to build up an imaginary picture of the cuisine of the Elves. Forget the Prancing Pony or the taverns of Minas Tirith—the best food to be had in Middle-earth is in the halls of the Elves. Eat, drink, and be merry!

Genealogy of the Races of Elves

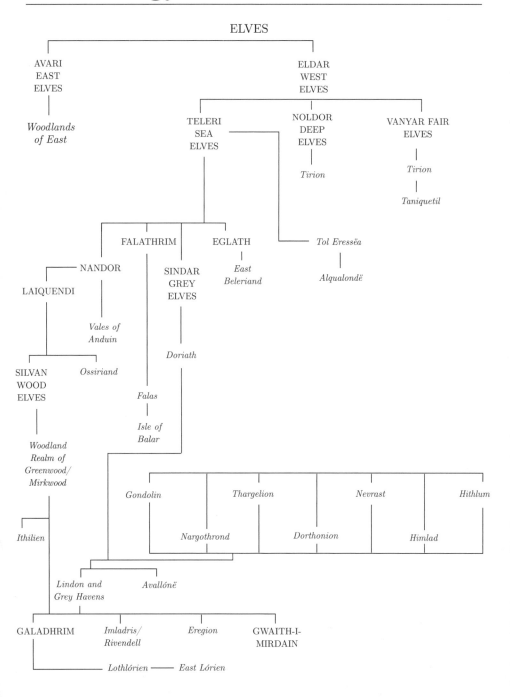

Breakfast Dishes

Whether or not breakfast is the most important meal of the day nutritionally, it can undoubtedly be one of the most significant emotionally. After breakfast often comes leave-taking and the beginning of a journey (even if it's just the commute to the office)—a cherished home and loved ones must, temporarily, be left behind.

It is a scenario that recurs frequently in *The Lord of the Rings*—the sweet sorrow of parting and the subsequent yearning for home are among its most enduring themes—and no doubt Tolkien's own leave-taking from his new wife, Edith, and departure for the Western Front in 1916, at the height of World War I, played a role here, too. The novel is punctuated by such heart-wrenching moments—Frodo's reluctant departure from the Shire; the Hobbits' leave-taking from the house of Tom Bombadil; the heavy-hearted departure of the Company of the Ring from Rivendell, and its subsequent, yet still heavier-hearted departure from the Elvish realm of Lothlórien—but, even so, breakfast is never quite forgotten. A long or difficult journey needs a well-filled stomach, after all.

So imagine yourself under the eaves of the Golden Wood, a long trip along the Great River is ahead of you—what would you choose for your breakfast as you bid farewell to the Elves and the beauty and safety of their realm?

Neldoreth Mushrooms

Woods and forests played an important role in Tolkien's imagination. The beechwoods of Neldoreth in the Beleriand—the vast homelands of the Elves in the First Age—provide a prototype for the enchanted woods we find in both *The Hobbit* (northern Mirkwood) and *The Lord of the Rings* (Lothlórien).

The primary association of Neldoreth, however, is with Lúthien, the most beautiful of the Elves, and a poetic incarnation of Tolkien's wife, Edith, with whom the author enjoyed many woodland walks. The love story of the Elf-maiden Lúthien and the mortal Beren haunted Tolkien through his life—a story that can be said to begin in Neldoreth where Beren first sees Lúthien dancing among the beech trees by moonlight.

Beechwoods in the fall are the perfect place for mushroom hunting, as any forager knows, and this simple dish will provide the perfect breakfast—whether we are in love or not.

Farl is traditional Irish potato bread and perfect for soaking up all the delicious garlicky mushroom cooking juices in this recipe. You could use thickly cut toasted whole-wheat bread instead.

Serves 2
Prep + cook time 30 minutes

1 tablespoon olive oil

2 tablespoons unsalted butter

2 shallots, finely chopped

3 cups mixed mushrooms, such as
    cremini, portobello, and button,
    trimmed and sliced

2 garlic cloves, chopped

1 tablespoon lemon juice

2 tablespoons chopped Italian parsley

2 extra-large eggs

4 ready-made potato farls, toasted

salt and pepper

1 tablespoon chopped chives,
    to garnish

1. Heat the oil with the butter in a skillet over high heat. Reduce the heat slightly, add the shallots and mushrooms, and fry for 6 minutes, stirring occasionally, until the mushrooms are golden. Stir in the garlic and cook, stirring, for 1 minute.

2. Add the lemon juice to the mushroom mixture and season with salt and pepper.

3. Remove the skillet from the heat and stir in the parsley. Keep warm while you poach the eggs.

4. Half-fill a separate skillet with water and bring to a simmer. Break in the eggs and cook for 3 minutes. Place two potato farls on each serving plate and top with the mushroom mixture, then the eggs. Sprinkle with the chives and serve immediately.

Tirion Tomatoes

Tolkien famously banished tomatoes from Middle-earth. In the first edition of *The Hobbit* (1927), during the 'unexpected party" with which the tale begins, Gandalf orders the poor, beleaguered Hobbit Bilbo Baggins to fetch cold chicken and tomatoes from his larder. By the third edition (1966), however, the 'tomatoes" had been replaced with 'pickles," since the fruit by now was considered an anachronism in Tolkien's conception of Middle-earth, which represents the Old World in a phase of its history many thousands of years before our own.

Side-stepping this thorny issue, we might indulgently imagine that Gandalf, in the original version, is recalling his former life as Olórin in Aman, the Blessed Realm—an America-like continent lying to the far west of Middle-earth, where both olvar (plants) and kelvar (animals) are different from those across the Great Sea. No doubt, tomatoes—the tomatl ('swelling fruit") of the Aztecs—were among the olvar of Aman and were a popular dish among the Eldar (High Elves) living there. Accordingly, we've named these delicious stuffed tomatoes for Tirion, the crystal-white city of Eldamar, the 'Elven-home" in Aman.

⌐—··—⌐

Stuffed with fresh herbs and soft cheese, these tomatoes are a great choice for brunch, served with buttered toast—try Yavanna's Whole-Wheat Bread on page 29. They're very forgiving so won't mind being left to cook in the oven for longer if you forget about them.

Serves 4
Prep + cook time 30 minutes

1 cup ricotta or cream cheese
2 scallions, finely chopped
4 tablespoons chopped mixed herbs,
    such as chervil, chives, parsley, basil,
    marjoram, and tarragon
finely grated rind of 1 lemon
1 tablespoon lemon juice
4 large beefsteak tomatoes
salt and pepper

1. For the herby ricotta filling, mix together the ricotta or cream cheese with the scallions, mixed herbs, and lemon rind and juice. Season with salt and pepper, and set aside.

2. Cut the tops off the tomatoes and scoop out the seeds. Stuff the tomatoes with the ricotta filling and transfer the tomatoes to a baking sheet. Bake in the oven at 375°F for 20–25 minutes, or until the tomatoes are tender.

Potato Rösti

There is something quintessentially Hobbitish about potatoes, of course. It's not just that Sam hankers after them in *The Lord of the Rings* and digs up "tatties" to make his famous rabbit stew out in the wilderness, but that their earthy wholesomeness seems to sum up everything the Shire is about. Think of potatoes in Tolkien, and we may well imagine Master Samwise or his old dad, the Gaffer, digging over the kitchen garden at Bag End, ready to plant the next seed crop. Potatoes, for Hobbits, clearly mean hearth, home, and happiness.

That doesn't mean to say, however, that the Elves are just too ethereal to eat the humble spud. They did not always live in fair cities or enchanted woodlands, after all. In *The Silmarillion*, Tolkien tells of the first awakening of the Elves in the far east of Middle-earth and the long journey westward of many of them in answer to the summons of the Valar. During that long trek, they endure many hardships, and they certainly wouldn't have turned their noses up at digging up a few tasty tubers to roast over their campfires. They could only have dreamed of the potato rösti here, though.

The Elven Cookbook

Originating in Switzerland as a simple two-ingredient peasant dish, a rösti is essentially a giant hash brown or potato fritter. Golden and crispy, it is great served with bacon, as here, or topped with a poached egg, or smoked salmon and sour cream.

Serves 4
Prep + cook time 40 minutes, plus cooling

3 potatoes, scrubbed but unpeeled, about 1¼ lb. total weight
½ onion, very thinly sliced
4 tablespoons vegetable oil
8 slices of bacon
salt and pepper

To serve
1 large bunch of watercress
1 avocado, peeled, pitted, and sliced (optional)

1. Cook the potatoes whole in a large saucepan of lightly salted boiling water for 8–10 minutes. Drain and set aside to cool. Once cooled, coarsely grate the potatoes and mix in a bowl with the sliced onion, 2 tablespoons of the oil, and plenty of salt and pepper.

2. Heat the remaining oil in a large nonstick skillet and add the rösti mixture, pushing down to flatten it so that it covers the base of the pan. Cook for 7–8 minutes, then slide onto an oiled plate or board. Flip the rösti back into the pan to cook the other side for 7–8 minutes until crisp and golden.

3. Meanwhile, fry the bacon and set aside to drain on some paper towels.

4. Cut the rösti into wedges, then arrange on serving plates, sprinkle with the watercress, and top with the bacon. Add some slices of avocado, if using, and serve immediately.

Beren's Vegan Scramble

We might call Beren, a scion of the House of Bëor, a kind of honorary Elf. He falls in love with the Elvish princess Lúthien, he is the forefather of the Peredhil—the Half-elves—including Elrond and Arwen, and his story is closely entwined with the tragic history of Beleriand and the Elvish struggle over the Silmarils (page 25). In his youth, he even lives like we might hope Elves would (though in reality they fall far short)—wandering free in the wilderness of Dorthonion, becoming close to the birds and animals, and refraining from eating meat. Since he is unlikely to have eaten cheese or eggs during this time (though there might have been wild honey to be had), he is as close to being a vegan as we can find in Tolkien's world.

This meatless breakfast dish, then, is for the greatest hero of the Edain in the First Age.

For a healthy and satisfying vegan take on scrambled eggs, try this protein-packed tofu and mushroom scramble. The mushroom ketchup adds a deep umami flavor to the dish. Serve it with hash browns or hot toast.

Serves 4
Prep + cook time 15 minutes

2 tablespoons canola or olive oil

2 cups cremini mushrooms, trimmed
  and quartered

1 cup firm tofu, drained, patted dry,
  and crumbled

1⅓ cups baby plum tomatoes, halved

1 tablespoon mushroom ketchup

3 tablespoons chopped Italian parsley

salt and pepper

1. Heat the oil in a skillet, add the mushrooms, and cook over high heat, stirring frequently, for 2 minutes until browned and softened. Add the tofu and cook, stirring, for 1 minute.

2. Add the tomatoes to the pan and cook for 2 minutes until starting to soften. Stir in the mushroom ketchup and half the parsley and season with salt and pepper.

3. Serve immediately, sprinkled with the remaining chopped parsley.

Bilbo's Rivendell Breakfast

We all know that Hobbits like their food, and that, of course, begins with breakfast. Bilbo Baggins and his compatriots would certainly concur with the old idea that we should "breakfast like a king." We might wonder and worry, then, how Bilbo fares when he goes into retirement in Rivendell, the hidden Elvish town in the foothills of the Misty Mountains, at the beginning of *The Lord of the Rings*. During his residence of almost two decades there he spends his days researching and recording Elvish lore and history (as well as writing down his own adventures), so he would have needed an especially hearty breakfast to prepare him for his day in Rivendell's ancient library.

Perhaps we needn't fret. Rivendell's ruler, Elrond, clearly has a soft spot for the aging Hobbit, and perhaps made sure that the Elvish cooks rustled up a good breakfast for him, like this one, with a good creamy cheese made from the milk of the secret valley's wild mountain goats.

This is a great recipe for a leisurely Sunday breakfast. The addition of mustard adds a piquant note to the omelette, which is filled with oozy melting goat cheese. Add some basil-speckled fried tomatoes for a more colorful plate.

Serves 4
Prep + cook time 30 minutes

4 tablespoons olive oil

3 cups mixed red and yellow cherry
 tomatoes, halved

a little basil, chopped, plus a few
 sprigs, to garnish

12 eggs

2 tablespoons whole-grain mustard

¼ cup butter

½ cup soft goat cheese, diced

salt and pepper

watercress, to garnish

1. Heat the oil in a skillet, add the tomatoes, and cook over medium heat for 2–3 minutes until softened (you may have to do this in two batches). Add the basil, season to taste with salt and pepper, then transfer to a bowl and keep warm.

2. Beat the eggs with the mustard in a large bowl and season with salt and pepper.

3. Melt 1 tablespoon of the butter in an omelette pan or small skillet over medium heat until it stops foaming, then swirl in a fourth of the egg mixture. Fork over the omelette so that it cooks evenly. As soon as it is set on the bottom (but still a little runny in the middle), dot over a quarter of the goat cheese, and cook for an additional 30 seconds. Carefully slide the omelette onto a plate, folding it in half as you do so. Keep warm.

4. Repeat with the remaining mixture to make three more omelettes. Serve with the tomatoes, garnished with watercress and basil sprigs.

Sirion Cured Salmon

Great rivers—the Nile, the Ganges, the Euphrates, the Mississippi—have always played an important role in human history as cradles of civilization and highways linking disparate territories and peoples. It's no surprise, then, to discover similar great rivers in Middle-earth. In *The Hobbit* and *The Lord of the Rings* it is the Anduin—the Great River of Wilderland—and in Beleriand, the lands of the Elves in *The Silmarillion*, it is the Sirion, another north–south flowing river that provides the unifying feature in a diverse landscape.

The Sirion makes repeated appearances in Tolkien's tales of Beleriand. Perhaps its closest association there is with the golden-haired Elven king Finrod—the older brother of Galadriel—who builds a guard tower, Minas Tirith, on Tol Sirion, the "island of Sirion," at the river's upper reaches. Finrod and his companions often wander along the banks of the Sirion, and though this recipe is an easy at-home cured version, we might well imagine them smoking their own freshly caught salmon from this wild, untamed river over their open campfires.

Served with scrambled eggs for a luxurious breakfast, cured salmon is delicious and a lot easier to make than you'd think. The basic recipe is equal parts salt and sugar plus flavorings—here coriander seeds and orange.

Serves 10 as a starter
Prep time 20 minutes, plus curing

1 lb. 2 oz. salmon fillet
¾ cup fine sea salt
1 cup light brown sugar
1 teaspoon black peppercorns
2 teaspoons coriander seeds
finely grated rind of 3 oranges

1. The day before you want to serve this, rinse the salmon fillet with cold water and pat it dry with paper towels.

2. Blitz the salt, sugar, peppercorns, coriander seeds, and orange rind in a food processor, then sprinkle roughly a third of the cure mix across the bottom of a shallow dish or plastic container big enough to hold the fish. Sit the salmon skin side down on the mixture, then top with the remaining cure, rubbing it all over. Cover the salmon with plastic wrap and leave in the refrigerator for 8–12 hours.

3. Remove from the refrigerator and rinse thoroughly with cold water, and pat dry with paper towels. If you get a chance, the fish will benefit from a couple of hours of extra drying time, left uncovered on a plate in the refrigerator. Slice thinly, starting from the widest end of the fillet, and serve.

Círdan's Golden Kedgeree

Not just for breakfast—you can tuck into this soothing fish, egg, and rice dish, with its mildly spicy curry flavor, any time of day. It makes a great winter brunch or dinner dish.

Serves 4
Prep + cook time 40 minutes

⅔ cup milk

½ cup cold water

1 bay leaf

14 oz. undyed smoked haddock

3 tablespoons boiling water

pinch of saffron threads

1 tablespoon vegetable oil

2 tablespoons butter

1 onion, finely chopped

1 garlic clove, finely chopped

1 teaspoon peeled and finely grated
   fresh ginger

1 teaspoon mild curry powder

1½ cups basmati rice

1 cup fish or vegetable stock

2 large eggs

5 tablespoons crème fraîche

salt and pepper

chopped Italian parsley, to garnish

1. Put the milk, measured cold water, and bay leaf in a shallow pan with a lid. Lay the haddock in the mixture, skin side down. Bring to a boil, cover, and simmer for 5 minutes, or until cooked through. Remove the haddock from the pan, reserving the milk mixture, and allow to cool.

2. Pour the measured boiling water over the saffron in a jug and leave to infuse.

3. Meanwhile, heat the oil and butter in a large saucepan. Add the onion and gently cook for 5 minutes until softened. Stir in the garlic and ginger, and cook for an additional 1 minute. Add the curry powder followed by the rice, and stir until well coated.

4. Stir in the reserved milk mixture, stock, and saffron with its soaking liquid. Bring to a boil, then leave to simmer for 15 minutes.

5. Meanwhile, bring a saucepan of water to a boil. Carefully lower in the eggs and cook for 3 minutes. Remove from the pan and cool under cold running water, then shell and cut into quarters.

6. Remove the skin from the cooled fish, flake into chunks, and add to the rice with the egg. Take off the heat, cover, and leave to stand for 5 minutes to warm through. Gently stir in the crème fraîche and season. Spoon onto plates and sprinkle with chopped parsley to serve.

The Sindarin Elf Círdan is one of the most enduring but also most elusive figures in Tolkien's legendarium, playing a part in all four ages in the history of Middle-earth. He makes his last appearance at the close of *The Lord of the Rings*, where he welcomes the Ring-bearers Frodo, Bilbo, Galadriel, and Gandalf to his realm of the Grey Havens (Mithlond), before they set off on their voyage into the West.

Throughout, Círdan's closest associations are with the sea and shipbuilding—his very name means "Shipwright"—and his people are known as the Falathrim—the "people of the shore." In myth, shipbuilders are often portrayed as being beacons of hope and having the gift of foresight—we have only to think of the biblical Noah and his ark—and Círdan persistently plays this role, even if he remains a largely shadowy figure.

This breakfast dish commemorates not only the shipwright's love of the sea but his role as the keeper of one of the three Elven rings, Narya, the Ring of Fire (page 79), before he later passes it on to Gandalf. Narya's flame color is mirrored in the gorgeous golden saffron used here.

114

Woodhall Apple Cake

One of the most enchanting moments in *The Lord of the Rings* is the Hobbits' early encounter with a wandering company of High Elves, led by Gildor Inglorion, at Woody End, a wild, wooded area close to the eastern border of the Shire. Part of the magic of this brief scene is that we seem to see it largely through the eyes of Sam, for whom it is his first meeting with the Fair Folk. The wonder of this happy meeting and the impromptu meal the Hobbits enjoy at Woodhall remains etched in his memory ever after.

He is above all enraptured by the Elves' singing but he also recalls the sweetness of the fruits they serve. He later wishes he could grow apples like those he tasted that night. The apple (Sindarin: *cordof*) seems to have a close association with the Elves, who in turn associate it in their tales and songs with the long-lost Entwives—the spirit-guardians of orchards and plants (page 144).

This super-easy and beautifully moist apple cake is perfect for breakfast or afternoon tea. You can ring the changes by replacing the lemon rind and juice with orange rind and juice, or replacing half the lemon rind and juice with lime.

Serves 10
Prep + cook time 1½ hours, plus cooling

1 cup dried apples, roughly chopped
⅓ cup water
¾ cup salted butter, softened
finely grated rind of 2 lemons
3 tablespoons lemon juice
¾ cup superfine sugar
3 eggs
2 cups self-rising flour
½ cup poppy seeds

For the icing
2 cups confectioners' sugar, sifted
1 tablespoon lemon juice

1. Put the apples and measured water in a small saucepan and heat for 5 minutes until the apples have absorbed the water. Leave to cool.

2. Beat together the remaining cake ingredients in a bowl until pale and creamy. Stir in the cooled apples.

3. Spoon the mixture into a greased and lined 8 x 4-inch loaf pan and level the surface. Bake in the oven at 325°F for 1–1¼ hours, or until firm to the touch and a skewer inserted into the center comes out clean. Loosen the cake at the ends and transfer to a wire rack. Peel off the lining paper and leave to cool.

4. Make the icing. Beat together the confectioners' sugar and lemon juice in a bowl to make a smooth, spoonable icing. If necessary, add a few drops of water or extra lemon juice. Spoon over the cake so that it runs down the sides.

Aman Cornbread Muffins

In Middle-earth, wheat seems to be the main cereal crop—both the Hobbits' homeland, the Shire, and the South-kingdom of the Dúnedain, Gondor (and no doubt other settled places inhabited by Men), seem to have plentiful wheat fields, and there is an abundance of reference to foods made from wheat, such as bread, cookies, and cakes. The Elves of Middle-earth grow wheat, too, though perhaps on a much smaller scale.

Wheat is also grown in Aman, the continent across the Sundering Sea. The New World crop now known in Europe as maize and in America as corn remains unmentioned, but we can well imagine it growing in abundance in the Undying Lands. In Pre-Columbian times, the cultivation of maize spread from southern Mexico across much of the Americas, and in Tolkien's world we might think of it being grown by the Vanyar, the fairest and noblest of the Elves who from even before the First Age dwelt exclusively in Aman. Their blond hair is certainly suggestive of golden corn fields and the brilliant sunshine color of the corncobs.

———··——

Whip up a batch of these cornbread muffins for a weekend breakfast treat to serve alongside crispy bacon, or scrambled or poached eggs. They're best eaten warm but also freeze well, and are great for picnics.

Makes 12
Prep + cook time 40 minutes

⅓ cup butter

1 large ear of corn, kernels sliced off

1 small onion, diced

½ red chili, deseeded and diced

1 cup all-purpose flour

1 cup cornmeal

2 teaspoons baking powder

½ cup grated cheddar cheese

pinch of salt

2 eggs

1 cup buttermilk

⅓ cup milk

1. Melt 2 tablespoons of butter in a saucepan over medium heat, add the corn, onion, and chilli, and cook for 2–3 minutes.

2. Sift together the flour, cornmeal, and baking powder. Stir in the grated cheddar and a pinch of salt.

3. Melt the remaining butter in a small saucepan. In a bowl, whisk together the eggs, melted butter, buttermilk, and milk. Stir the wet ingredients into the dry, add the corn mixture, and mix lightly. Divide between the holes of a greased 12-hole muffin pan.

4. Bake in the oven at 375°F for 18–20 minutes until golden and cooked through.

Silmaril Breakfast Friands

The *Silmarillion*—Tolkien's account of the First Age—takes its name from the Silmarils—three jewels created by the proud Noldor Elf Fëanor, filled with the light of the Two Trees of Valinor. Of extraordinary beauty, the Silmarils provide a leitmotif for the tales, as they are coveted and fought over by Elves, Men, Dwarves, and the Dark Lord Morgoth—in an epic struggle that culminates in the War of the Jewels and the catastrophic destruction of Beleriand. The jewels—both miraculous and seemingly cursed—play a similar role to the Necklace of Harmonia in the downfall of Thebes in Greek mythology, or the Brísingamen necklace in Norse legends and tales.

These delicate breakfast friands, studded with jewel-like fruit, may not be quite as transcendently beautiful as the legendary Silmarils, but they may well have the power to create dissension around the breakfast table over who will get the last one!

continued on the following page ⇥

Made with egg whites and very little flour, these fruit-spiked friands are beautifully light while the ground almonds ensure they are moist and just the right kind of chewy. Delicious with a cup of coffee for an indulgent breakfast.

Makes 12
Prep + cook time 40 minutes, plus cooling

¾ cup unsalted butter

3 oz. dried strawberries, sour cherries, or cranberries, roughly chopped

2 tablespoons orange juice

6 egg whites

1 cup superfine sugar, plus extra for sprinkling

⅔ cup all-purpose flour

1 cup ground almonds

1. Melt the butter and leave to cool. Put the strawberries, cherries, or cranberries and orange juice in a saucepan and heat until the mixture is hot, then turn into a bowl and leave to cool.

2. Whisk the egg whites in a large, clean bowl with a handheld electric whisk until frothy and increased in volume but not peaking. Add the sugar, flour, and ground almonds and stir in until almost combined. Drizzle the melted butter over the mixture, then stir together gently until just combined.

3. Divide the mixture evenly between the holes of a greased 12-hole muffin pan, then sprinkle the strawberries, cherries, or cranberries on top. Bake in the oven at 400°F for about 20 minutes until pale golden and just firm to the touch. Leave in the pan for 5 minutes, then transfer to a wire rack to cool. Serve sprinkled with superfine sugar.

Teiglin Roast Hazelnut Muesli

In his creation of Middle-earth, Tolkien developed an especially rich and elaborate flora, encompassing both real-world species (or relatives thereof) and imaginary ones. Thus, alongside tree species such as oak and beech, we also find entirely fictional ones such as the kingly mallorn, which flourishes in Lothlórien. Whatever their origin—in nature or fancy—Tolkien describes them in loving detail, so that as we walk about the Shire with the Hobbits or wander about Beleriand with the heroes of *The Silmarillion*, we develop a deep appreciation for Middle-earth's landscapes and the living things that dwell in them.

One especially common real-world species we comes across in Middle-earth is the hazel, or filbert. In Beleriand, it is depicted growing in stands about the wooded banks of the River Teiglin—a tributary of the Sirion (page 19) and its nuts, which become especially sweet when roasted, were no doubt eaten by both Elves and Men alike.

———··———

Full of good things and no nasties, homemade muesli makes sure you start your day the right way. You can vary the dried fruit: try dried cranberries or apricots, chopped dates, goji berries, or currants.

Serves 4
Prep + cook time 25 minutes, plus cooling

1 cup shredded dried coconut
1 cup slivered almonds
¾ cup blanched hazelnuts
¾ cup sunflower seeds
1½ cups buckwheat groats
2 cups millet flakes
1 cup dried mango, sliced
¾ cup golden raisins

1. Spread the coconut out in a thin layer on a baking sheet. Spread the slivered almonds, hazelnuts, and sunflower seeds out in a thin layer on a second baking sheet. Toast in the oven at 300°F for about 20 minutes, stirring every 5 minutes to make sure it browns evenly. Keep a close eye on the sunflower seeds and don't let them burn.

2. Remove the trays from the oven and leave to cool, then roughly chop the hazelnuts.

3. Mix the toasted mixture with all the remaining ingredients in a large bowl until well combined. Store in an airtight container for up to two weeks.

Yavanna's Whole-Wheat Bread

In *The Silmarillion*, wheat is described growing tall and golden in the fields of Yavanna in Valinor, the realm of the Valar—the great spirits who helped form Arda (the Earth) after its creation. For Tolkien, Valinor—a part of the continent of Aman—was clearly closely akin to the lands of plenty that abound in the world's mythologies—from the Vanaheimr of the Norse myths, home to the Vana, gods of fertility, to the Cockaigne of medieval legend. It is tempting to draw comparisons, too, with the legends that quickly grew up around the Americas after the first arrival of Europeans in the late fifteenth century—as a continent blessed with oversized fruits and vegetables and a superabundance of game.

The nurturing figure of Yavanna herself is heavily indebted to mythological goddesses such as the Greek Demeter, the Roman Ceres, and the Norse Sif, all closely associated with the grain harvest, though Yavanna's remit as Tolkien's "Mother Earth" runs to all living creatures and plants. Nurture yourself by making this wholesome loaf made from the "ancient grain" known as spelt and imagine yourself breakfasting looking out over the blissful, sunny landscapes of Valinor.

Is there anything better than the aroma of freshly baked bread? Needing no proofing time and no kneading, this sunflower-studded loaf is super-quick to rustle up for a weekend breakfast. Serve warm with butter and a dollop of Ithilien Bramble Jelly (see page 32).

Makes 1 loaf
Prep + cook time 1 hour

2 cups all-purpose flour, plus extra for
   dusting
1½ cups whole-wheat spelt flour
1 cup rye flour
2 teaspoons baking powder
1 teaspoon salt
½ cup sunflower seeds, plus
   2 tablespoons
2 cups plain yogurt
milk, to glaze

1. Mix together the flours, baking powder, salt, and ½ cup of sunflower seeds in a bowl. Stir in the yogurt and mix to a fairly soft dough.

2. Shape the dough into a log on a floured surface, then drop into a greased 8 x 4-inch loaf pan. Brush with a little milk and sprinkle with the remaining sunflower seeds.

3. Bake in the oven at 425°F for 20 minutes. Reduce the oven temperature to 325°F and bake for an additional 30 minutes. The base of the bread should sound hollow when tapped. If necessary, return to the oven for a little longer. Transfer to a wire rack to cool.

Gondolin Rose-Petal Jelly

Hidden mountain kingdoms are a common motif in myth and legend—from the utopian Shambhala of East Asian Buddhism to the fabled city of gold El Dorado, long searched for by the Spanish conquistadors. In Tolkien, the quintessential hidden kingdom is Gondolin, founded just after the beginning of the First Age by the Noldorin lord Turgon. Hidden within the Encircling Mountains, in the north of Beleriand, it can be reached only by a closely guarded Hidden Way.

In his voluminous notes, Tolkien imagined Gondolin in some detail—its gates, streets, squares, and buildings. It was renowned for its marble houses and its flower gardens, and especially, it seems, for its fragrant roses. The Alley of Roses, close to the king's palace, is noted as an especially beautiful place to walk in. The city was destroyed by the forces of Morgoth in FA 510, a catastrophe recounted as one of the so-called Great Tales told in *The Silmarillion* and in *The Fall of Gondolin*. Recapture something of the lost beauty of this hidden Noldorin kingdom in this fragrant rose-petal jelly.

Delicate and lightly fragrant, this softly set jelly is lovely on hot crumpets, swirled into thick yogurt, or spooned over oatmeal. It's important to make it with rose petals that haven't been sprayed with any kind of chemical. The rose petals may lose their color during the cooking process, but don't panic—the lemon juice will restore the color!

Makes 3 jars
Prep + cook time 50 minutes

1 cup water
2½ oz. unsprayed rose petals, washed
2 cups granulated sugar
3 tablespoons lemon juice
1 teaspoon pectin

1. Place the measured water and rose petals in a saucepan over low heat and simmer gently for 10 minutes. Add 1½ cups of the sugar and stir to dissolve the sugar crystals. Add the lemon juice and simmer for an additional 10 minutes.

2. Meanwhile, mix the remaining sugar and pectin in a small bowl. Add to the jelly a little at time, stirring constantly to make sure the pectin doesn't clump. Simmer for an additional 20 minutes.

3. The jelly will still be quite runny—it will firm up as it sets and cools but the texture stays syrupy rather than thick.

4. Ladle into sterilized, warm, dry jars. Cover with screw-top lids and leave to cool. The jelly will keep for up to two months in the fridge or it can be frozen for up to six months.

Ithilien Bramble Jelly

As any rambler knows, brambles—blackberries—can be both a pleasure and a nuisance. The fruit is a sweet juicy treat for the walker, but gathering in great thorny thickets can offer a prickly hindrance along the path. In Tolkien's Mordor, the blighted land of Sauron, there are even "super-brambles," with knifelike thorns, which bear more than a passing resemblance to the concertina barbed-wire fences experienced by Tolkien and many other soldiers during World War I.

The Brambles of Mordor's rather gentler cousins are also shown growing in Ithilien, the once-fair land to the east of Gondor that has been blighted by the evildoings of Sauron and the Morgul-king. After the end of the War of the Rings, the Sindarin Elf Legolas settles with some of his people in Ithilien and works to restore its woodlands to their former glory. It would be nice to think that the bramble—usually a sign of neglect—would not be entirely banished and that—tamed and tended—would be used by the Elves to make a wonderful jelly much like this one.

⌐——••••——⌐

The trickiest part of making jelly is knowing when it has reached setting point. An easy way to tell is to drop a teaspoon of jelly onto a saucer that's been chilled in the refrigerator or freezer. The jelly will quickly cool to room temperature. Push the jelly gently with your finger—the skin will wrinkle if it's ready. If it's not, return the jelly to the heat, boil it again, and retest in a few minutes.

Makes 4 jars
Prep + cook time 50 minutes

3 cups blackberries

9 figs, quartered

1 cup water

2 cinnamon sticks, halved

4 cups granulated sugar, warmed

juice of 1 lemon

1 tablespoon butter (optional)

1. Add the blackberries and figs to a large saucepan. Pour in the measured water, then add the cinnamon sticks. Bring to a simmer, then simmer, uncovered, for about 10 minutes, until the fruit is just beginning to soften.

2. Pour the sugar into the pan and add the lemon juice. Heat gently, stirring from time to time, until the sugar has dissolved. Bring to a boil, then boil rapidly until setting point is reached (see above)—about 25 minutes. Skim with a draining spoon, or stir in butter if needed (this will help to break up any foamy scum on the surface).

3. Ladle into sterilized, warm, dry jars, filling to the very top and discarding the cinnamon sticks. Cover with screw-top lids, or with waxed discs and cellophane tops secured with elastic bands. Label and leave to cool.

Arwen's Bilberry Jelly

Bilberries seem to grow in thickets in the foothills of the Misty Mountains: in *The Lord of the Rings*, Aragorn and the four Hobbits seek refuge from the Black Riders in the deep heather and bilberry brushwood as they hazard the final stretch to Rivendell along the Great East–West Road. We may well imagine, then, that bilberries are one of the popular gathered fruits of the Rivendell Elves, made into jellies and compotes or as an accompaniment to roasted meats.

This delicious bilberry jelly might be a particular favorite of Aragorn, a treat made and served by the Half-Elven Arwen Undómiel to her betrothed on one of his rare visits to her father's realm. Even weather-beaten heroes like a few simple pleasures in their lives.

This easy-to-make berry jelly uses frozen blueberries for convenience and is perfect with hot scones or toast. For a grown-up spin, you can stir a teaspoon of whiskey or gin into each jar of jelly before covering and storing.

Makes 4–5 jars
Prep + cook time 30 minutes

2 x 15¼-oz. packs frozen blueberries
3 cups fresh raspberries
4 cups jam sugar with pectin
1 tablespoon butter (optional)

1. Add the frozen blueberries and the raspberries to a large saucepan. Cover and cook gently for 10 minutes, stirring from time to time, until the juices run and the fruit begins to soften.

2. Pour the sugar into the pan and heat gently, stirring from time to time, until dissolved. Bring to a boil, then boil rapidly until setting point is reached (see page 32)—about 5–10 minutes. Skim with a draining spoon, or stir in butter if needed (this will help to break up any foamy scum on the surface).

3. Ladle into sterilized, warm, dry jars, filling to the very top. Cover with screw-top lids, or with waxed discs and cellophane tops secured with elastic bands. Label and leave to cool.

Edhellond Almond Butter

The haven of Edhellond was the most southerly settlement of the Sindarin Elves in Middle-earth, founded by refugees from war-torn Beleriand during the First Age. It is the setting of the tragic finale of one of Tolkien's saddest love stories, the story of Amroth, king of Lothlórien, and the Elf-maid Nimrodel. By the time of the events narrated in *The Lord of the Rings*, the haven has long since been abandoned, though the mortal rulers of the surrounding lands, the Princes of Dol Amroth, are said to have Elvish blood, being descendants of a Númenórean lord and one of Nimrodel's companions, Mithrellas.

Edhellond, like the kingdom of Gondor of which in the Third Age it became a part, would have enjoyed a warm, sunny, Mediterranean-type climate, perfect for the cultivation of almond trees, with their glorious pinkish-white blossoms. It is perfectly possible, then, that the Elves of Edhellond made something akin to this delicious almond butter, and that they later passed the secret of its making to the Gondorians, passed down the line of the Princes of Dol Amroth.

Homemade nut butter is healthy, cheap, uncomplicated to make, and tastes so much better than anything you can buy. Add honey or maple syrup, a hint of vanilla extract, and a pinch of cinnamon to make it extra-special, if you like.

Makes 10 oz.
Prep + cook time 20 minutes

2 cups skin-on almonds
drizzle of honey or maple syrup
few drops of vanilla extract (optional)
ground cinnamon, to taste (optional)

1. Spread the almonds evenly on a baking tray and roast in the oven at 375°F for about 10 minutes, making sure to turn them or give them a toss halfway through. Be careful not to let the nuts burn. Remove from the oven and leave to cool.

2. Put the almonds into a food processor and blitz for 10 minutes, stopping every now and then to scrape down the sides with a spatula if necessary. When the almonds are your desired consistency, add the honey or maple syrup, and vanilla extract and cinnamon, if using, and blitz for another 30 seconds until well combined.

3. Store in a sealed container in the refrigerator for up to three weeks.

Radagast's Homemade Oat Milk

We know that the Elves of the Great Greenwood (Mirkwood) were far from being vegetarian, but this oat milk may well have delighted them when, passing south to visit their kindred in Lothlórien, they were treated to a glass of it at Rhosgobel, the home of the wizard Radagast the Brown. In Valinor he was a Maia in the service of Yavanna, and on his mission to Middle-earth was especially concerned with its animals and plants. We know nothing of his dietary habits, but he is unlikely to have been a meat-eater as we know Gandalf to have been—so this oat milk might have been just the thing for him to make. The oats, of course, would have been traded through his Northmen neighbors, the Beornings.

⌐—··⌐

Making your own oat milk allows you to control the ingredients and is very easy to do. You can customize it to suit your taste by adding a dash of vanilla extract, a couple of dates, or a little maple syrup or honey to sweeten.

Makes about 26 fl. oz.
Prep time 20 minutes, plus soaking and straining

1 cup rolled oats
2½ cups cold water
pinch of salt

1. Put the oats into a bowl and add water to cover them. Cover and set aside somewhere cool for 4 hours or overnight.

2. Strain the oats, discarding the soaking water. Add the oats to a food processor, along with the measured cold water and the salt. Blend until completely smooth and there are no pieces of oat visible.

3. Line a strainer with clean cheesecloth and place over a bowl or jug. Pour in the oat milk, then leave to strain for 1 hour, or until most of the liquid has drained into the bowl or jug. Gather together the sides of the cheesecloth and squeeze tightly to extract the last of the milk.

4. Pour the milk into a bottle and store in the refrigerator. This will keep for two or three days.

Elvish Cuisines

◦━━•••━━◦

We can conjecture that there was not a single Elvish cuisine but many. The diasporic spread of Tolkien's Elves from the far east of Middle-earth—where they first appeared—to its western regions and shores, and from there across the sea to Aman, together with the vast ages that passed between their Awakening and the "present" of *The Lord of the Rings*, would have ensured that a wealth of cooking styles and preferences evolved, at least as complex as the evolution of the Elvish kindreds (page 9). We can thus be pretty sure, for example, that the shore-dwelling and seafaring Teleri ate a fish-based diet, that the forest-dwelling Sindar consumed a lot of game and berries, and that the Noldor of, say, the city of Gondolin in Beleriand made good use of the produce of their farms, orchards, and kitchen gardens.

Just as in human history, there would also have been a progression from relatively basic methods of cooking to more or less sophisticated ones. No doubt the "primitive" Elves of Cuiviénen (the place where the Elves first awoke) all cooked in much the same way—over an open fire and using the simplest of gathered and hunted ingredients from sea and forest—but by the time of the First Age the Eldar at least must have developed more civilized cooking methods. They no doubt had ovens and a panoply of kitchen equipment at their disposal, and used produce they themselves had grown or reared, having been taught the arts of agriculture by the Valar, the Maiar, and the Ent-wives. This development, however, would never have been clear cut or absolute. The Elves of Lothlórien or Rivendell—the "latest" Elves we meet in the pages of Tolkien's books—no doubt never entirely gave up on their ancient hunter-gatherer ways and continued to cook, at least at times, over open fires, as indeed occurs in *The Hobbit* where there seems to be a contrast made between the food on offer down in the woods and that being served up in Elrond's halls.

For all this variety and difference, all this evolution, however, perhaps it is possible to speak of an Elvish cuisine in the singular—of characteristics that unite the way in which Elves cooked and ate across vast lengths of time and space, different from those of Men, Dwarves, and Hobbits. We might, of course, pinpoint a preference for the fresh, the seasonal and the local—a diet that is as close to nature as can be—a diet, moreover,

of moderation and lightness that works in harmony with the body and not against it, with the power to energize, not dissipate—but something more, too—the *je ne sais quoi* that elevates the extraordinary above the ordinary. Perhaps this is captured best early on in *The Lord of the Rings* when Frodo, Pippin, and Sam eat an al fresco Elvish meal at Woody End, where, at least in the memory of the Hobbits, everything tastes at once dreamlike and yet more intense, more vivid, than anything they have tasted before.

Light Meals

Although several times in *The Hobbit* and *The Lord of the Rings* we catch the Elves dining on roasted meat or drinking heavy red wines, we are more likely to associate these ethereal beings with lighter fare than the heartier meals enjoyed, say, by Hobbits and Dwarves. To use French terminology, we would probably think of their culinary preferences as leaning more towards *cuisine minceur* ("lean cuisine") than *cuisine bourgeoise*. How else could Tolkien's Elves be so uniformly slender, fit, and healthy?

The archetypal Elvish meal, then, may be that provided to the Hobbits by the Noldorin Elf Gildor in Woody End in the Shire in Chapter 3 of *The Lord of the Rings*—light, fresh, fragrant . . . and memorable. Of the meal of bread, vegetables, fruits, and drink brought by the Elves to the hall-like clearing, Pippin afterward recalled that he felt as though he was in a "waking dream." Perhaps we cannot promise quite that effect with the recipes on offer in this section, but we hope to capture something of the Elvish spirit—food that leaves you feeling nourished but not overfull; food that uses simple ingredients, simply prepared, food that is, above all, memorable for you and your guests.

Greenwood Nettle Soup

Nettles grow abundantly in the woods and wild places of Middle-earth:
Tolkien quite often mentions them, sometimes in association with other
rampant, stinging, scratching, or even toxic species such as thistle and hemlock.
In the Old Forest, for example, such weedlike species are used symbolically,
connoting a wilder, more dangerous world than the safety of the neighboring
Shire, with its cultivated fields of mushrooms, oats, tobacco, and wheat.

We may well imagine, however, that the Elves, especially those known as the
Laiquendi ("Green-elves"), who live in the woodlands of Middle-earth, knew
how to make good use of nettles and of the rich source of vitamins and protein
they contain—especially in the spring when the shoots are young and tender.
Here, then, is a tasty soup that might have been made on a sunny spring day
in the woodlands of Ossiriand or Greenwood the Great (Mirkwood).

*This tasty dark green soup makes the most of foraged nettles. For extra luxury,
top with a swirl of thick cream before serving. Be sure to wear gloves when
handling the nettles and wash them well in cold water before adding to the soup.*

Serves 6
Prep + cook time 1 hour

2 tablespoons butter

1 onion, roughly chopped

1 baking potato, about 8 oz., diced

3 cups vegetable or chicken stock

¼ teaspoon grated nutmeg

4½ cups nettle leaves, well washed
    and drained

1 cup milk

salt and pepper

1. Heat the butter in a saucepan, add the onion,
   and fry gently for 5 minutes until softened.
   Add the potato, cover, and cook for 10 minutes,
   stirring occasionally.

2. Pour in the stock, add the nutmeg, and salt and
   pepper, then bring to a boil. Cover and simmer for
   20 minutes until the potato is soft. Add the nettle
   leaves to the pan. Re-cover the pan and cook for
   5 minutes until just wilted.

3. Puree the soup in batches in a blender or food
   processor until smooth, then pour back into the
   saucepan, mix in the milk, gently
   reheat, and serve.

Kine of Araw's Oxtail Soup

During the earliest ages of Arda, Oromë, the Huntsman of the Valar, spends much of his time away from the splendors of Valinor, hunting the dark creatures of Melkor/Morgoth in the benighted continent of Middle-earth. Associated with him, in Elven lore, are the colossal, majestic cattle known as the Kine of Araw that roamed the eastern regions—Araw being the Vala's name in Sindarin.

The kine seem to be closely related to the sun (though the sun did not yet exist in earliest times). Tolkien describes their flanks as brilliant white, reflecting the sunlight at the Gates of Morning in the east—a detail that may relate to the cattle of the sun god Helios in Greek mythology. This deep-bodied soup might have been made by the Elves on winter days when they dreamed of their lost home in Valinor and the Valar and kindred who lived there.

Rich and comforting, this is the perfect meal when it's gray and cold outside. It improves with keeping, so any leftovers will be even better the following day. For a complete feast, serve with the Cornbread Muffins on page 24.

Serves 6
Prep + cook time 5 hours

1 tablespoon sunflower oil

5 cups oxtail pieces, string removed

1 onion, finely chopped

2 carrots, diced

2 celery sticks, diced

1½ cups potatoes, diced

small bunch of mixed herbs

2 cups beef stock

1½ cups strong ale

2 teaspoons English mustard

2 tablespoons Worcestershire sauce

1 tablespoon tomato paste

13½-oz. can lima beans, rinsed and drained

salt and pepper

chopped parsley, to garnish

1. Heat the oil in a large saucepan, add the oxtail pieces, and fry until browned on one side. Turn the oxtail pieces over and add the onion, stirring until browned on all sides. Stir in the carrots, celery, potatoes, and herbs and cook for an additional 2–3 minutes.

2. Pour in the stock and ale, then add the mustard, Worcestershire sauce, tomato paste, and lima beans. Season well with salt and pepper and bring to a boil, stirring. Half-cover the pan and simmer gently for 4 hours.

3. Lift the oxtail and herbs out of the pan with a slotted spoon. Discard the herbs and cut the meat off the oxtail bones, discarding any fat. Return the meat to the pan, reheat gently, then taste and adjust the seasoning if needed. Ladle into bowls and sprinkle with the chopped parsley.

Alqualondëan Clam Soup

The principal city of Tol Eressëa (see page 45) is Alqualondë, which, despite its watery-sounding toponym, means 'Swanhaven'—named for the beautiful swan-shaped ships moored in its harbors. Its buildings, Tolkien tells us, are studded with pearls and the city is lit by many lamps.

Tolkien does not tell us what kind of pearl the Elves used to decorate their city, but perhaps they were clam, rather than oyster, pearls, and so may have been a by-product of Elvish clam fishing. Pearls from giant clams (genus *Tridacna*) can be exceptionally large—as in the famous Pearl of Lao Tzu, which is 9½ inches in diameter—and so would have provided good food as well as fine decoration.

⌐ ⋯ ⌐

Bursting with flavor and texture from the lardoons, potatoes, and clams, this hearty and creamy soup is a complete meal in a bowl. Be sure to discard any clams that are still closed after cooking.

Serves 4
Prep + cook time 45 minutes

1 tablespoon butter

1 tablespoon vegetable oil

½ cup lardoons

1 onion, finely chopped

1 red chili, finely chopped

⅓ cup dry white wine

2 cups milk

1 cup heavy cream

⅔ cups chicken stock

3 cups baby potatoes, halved

1 lb. cleaned live clams

handful of chopped Italian parsley,
    to garnish

1. Heat the butter and vegetable oil in a skillet. Add the lardoons and cook for about 5 minutes until golden brown. Remove from the pan. Add the onion and cook for about 7 minutes until softened.

2. Stir in the chili and return the lardoons to the pan. Pour in the wine and boil for about 2 minutes until reduced. Pour in the milk, heavy cream, and chicken stock and bring to a boil.

3. Stir through the baby potatoes and cook for 10 minutes or until tender. Add the clams. Cover and cook for 5 minutes until the clams have opened, discarding any that remain closed.

4. Sprinkle with a handful of chopped Italian parsley and serve.

Tol Eressëa Samphire Sea Salad

Tolkien was no stranger to plundering the world's mythologies to enrich his own, and one such flotsam of his plunder is Tol Eressëa—the floating island of Belegaer, the vast ocean between the two great continents of Middle-earth and Aman. In Homer's *Odyssey* we find the floating island of Aeolia—the Isle of the Winds—and in Celtic legend Tír na nÓg—an elusive paradise floating somewhere off the Irish coast, appearing and disappearing in the Atlantic mists.

Tolkien's own floating island is used as an actual boat. Originally, the island was attached to the ocean floor, but after the Valar summon the Elves to Aman, the Vala of the sea, Ulmo, uproots the island and uses it as a giant vessel to transport the three kindreds across the ocean. Later, the island is once again anchored to the ocean floor, just off Aman, and becomes the home of the Teleri, the Sea-elves.

On their voyage across Belegaer, the Elves would surely have used the natural produce of their island-raft, foraging what they could from its shores. This fresh-tasting sea salad has as its principal ingredient samphire, which grows abundantly in salt marshes.

This salad is full of intense summer flavors and makes a lovely lunch on a hot day. Use really ripe tomatoes and be aware of samphire's inherent saltiness when seasoning—you won't need a lot of extra salt.

Serves 4
Prep time 15 minutes, plus standing

4 cups large tomatoes, roughly chopped into ¾-inch pieces
1 teaspoon sea salt
1½ cups samphire, trimmed
5 oz. ciabatta bread
½ red onion, finely chopped
handful of basil leaves, plus extra to garnish
1 tablespoon red wine vinegar
2 tablespoons extra-virgin olive oil
salt and pepper

1. Put the chopped tomatoes into a nonmetallic bowl and sprinkle with the sea salt. Leave to stand for an hour.

2. Meanwhile, bring a saucepan of water to a boil, add the samphire, and blanch for 1 minute. Drain the samphire and immediately place in a bowl of iced water. Drain and pat dry with paper towels.

3. Remove the crusts from the ciabatta and tear into rough chunks.

4. Give the tomatoes a good squash with clean hands, then add the samphire, ciabatta, onion, basil, vinegar, and oil, and season to taste with salt and pepper. Mix together carefully, then sprinkle with the remaining basil, and serve.

Menegroth Endive and Pear Salad

It is not only Tolkien's Dwarves who build subterranean kingdoms but his Elves, too. The most famous of these is the capital of the forest kingdom of Doriath, Menegroth—the city of a Thousand Caves, hewn deep into the side of a ravine. But there are other underground Elvish kingdoms and fortresses, too—Nargothrond, the stronghold of the Noldorin Elf lord Finrod, modeled on Menegroth; and, in *The Hobbit*, the subterranean halls of the Elvenking (Thranduil), who originally came from Doriath. In associating some of his Elves with such chthonic cities, Tolkien is probably alluding to the dark-elves—*dökkálfar*—of Norse mythology who, unlike the *ljósálfar* (light-elves), live underground and seem to be (like some of Tolkien's Elves indeed) gifted smiths.

Dark and light come together in this tasty salad. Belgian endive, or witloof, is a sprouted chicory root grown indoors without sunlight and so might be thought uniquely suited to the Elves' cavernous kingdoms. Here it is teamed, however, with fragrant pears and rose petals—thus also associating it with the rose-garlanded Lúthien, bright daughter of Doriath's dark-browed king, Thingol.

⌖

This unconventional and very pretty Moroccan-inspired salad pairs crisp, mildly bitter endive with ripe pears steeped in rosewater. You don't have to use the rose petals but their aromatic, sweet flavor adds an extra dimension to this summery salad.

Serves 4
Prep time 10 minutes

2 ripe but firm pears, peeled, cored, and thinly sliced

juice of ½ lemon

1–2 tablespoons rosewater

2 heads of white or Belgian endive, leaves separated and rinsed

1 tablespoon olive oil

1 teaspoon runny honey

small handful of fresh, scented rose petals

salt

1. Place the pears in a bowl and lightly toss with the lemon juice and rosewater. Leave to stand for 5 minutes.

2. Arrange the endive leaves in a shallow salad bowl. Remove the pear from the rosewater and lemon juice with a slotted spoon, and sprinkle it over and around the endive leaves.

3. Mix the oil with any rosewater and lemon juice left in the bowl and pour over the salad. Drizzle over the honey and sprinkle with salt. Sprinkle with the rose petals and toss just before serving.

Silverlode Smoked Trout

Tolkien spent the happiest years of his childhood in the hamlet of Sarehole (then in Worcestershire and now part of Birmingham) and fondly remembered playing on the banks of the small river that ran through it, the Cole. The Cole and Sarehole's busy watermill became the model for the Water and the Old Mill in the Shire, both seen prominently in his charming watercolor illustration *The Hill: Hobbiton-across-the-Water*, included in some editions of *The Hobbit*.

It is not surprising, then, that rivers large and small, tributaries, and streams played such an important role in Tolkien's imagination and in his geography of Middle-earth, and are always given evocative names—the Withywindle, the Brandywine, Greyflood, Entwash . . . the Silverlode (Celebrant in Sindarin) seems a more than appropriate name for the small river that runs from near the East-gate of the Dwarven mansions of Moria, through the Elven woodland realm of Lothlórien, and finally into the Anduin, the Great River. It evokes at once the fast-flowing waters of the Silverlode itself, the diamond-hard, silver-colored metal mithril mined in Moria, the white garments of Galadriel, Lothlórien's Elven-queen, possessor of the White Ring, Nenya . . . and perhaps, too, the silvery rainbow trout that might, we imagine, swim along its length.

Smoked trout has a more delicate flavor than the commonly used smoked salmon and pairs beautifully with the sweetness of the grapes in this salad. Serve it as an elegant starter or light lunch.

Serves 2
Prep time 15 minutes

7 oz. smoked trout
1 cup red seedless grapes
1 bunch watercress
1 fennel bulb

For the dressing
3 tablespoons mayonnaise
4 cornichons, finely diced
1½ tablespoons capers, chopped
2 tablespoons lemon juice
salt and pepper

1. Flake the smoked trout into bite-size pieces, removing any bones, and place in a large salad bowl. Wash and drain the grapes and watercress, then add them to the bowl. Finely slice the fennel bulb and add to the mix.

2. Make the dressing by mixing the mayonnaise, cornichons, capers, and lemon juice. Season to taste with salt and pepper, then carefully mix through the salad, and serve.

Seaweed Cakes

Many of Tolkien's "gods"—his Valar and Maiar—bear more than a passing resemblance to those of ancient real-world mythologies. Uinen, a Maia in the service of Ulmo, Lord of the Waters, has a close affinity with such figures as the Greek sea goddess Leucothea, who in Homer's *Odyssey* saves its shipwrecked hero, Odysseus, from drowning—quite apart from her associations with the mermaids of folklore (at least the kindly ones among them). Unlike her unruly husband, Ossë, who is forever whipping up storms, Uinen represents the more beneficent aspects of the sea—calm sunlit waters, the fruitful shore, and salt streams. The Teleri of the coasts of Beleriand had an especially close relationship with Uinen, as did the seafaring Men of Númenor, who prayed for her help out at sea.

Here we have imagined little sushi parcels that the Teleri prepared and ate in honor of Uinen, the wrappings made from the tangled masses of seaweed they gathered from the rock pools close to their havens and whose strands reminded them of the long hair of the Maia herself.

⟢ ⋯ ⟣

A picture on a plate, these little seaweed cakes are less fiddly to prepare than traditional rolled sushi but just as tasty. Serve with soy sauce and fiery wasabi for dipping and, if you like, some pickled ginger to accompany them.

Serves 4
Prep time 20 minutes

3 cups cooked sushi rice

sushi rice seasoning, to taste

4 sheets of nori seaweed

3½ oz. smoked salmon

⅓ cup cucumber, very thinly sliced

To serve

soy sauce

wasabi

1. Season the rice with the sushi rice seasoning.

2. Place two of the seaweed sheets on a board. Spread a quarter of the rice over each, cover with the smoked salmon, then the cucumber. Spoon over the remaining rice, then top with the other seaweed sheets. Press the sushi down well so the layers stick together.

3. Cut into four triangles and serve with soy sauce and wasabi.

Lindon Potted Crab

Tolkien thought of Middle-earth as a kind of other-Europe—a Europe of a mythologized time and dimension long before—and outside of—the present day. The famous map of Middle-earth was, to some degree, calqued on that of Europe, with the Shire, for example, corresponding to the English West Midlands and Minas Tirith to Mediterranean Rome. But what of Beleriand, the Elvish lands of the First Age that, at the close of *The Silmarillion*, are largely submerged beneath the ocean but whose remnants—Forlindon and Harlindon—lie, at the time of the events of *The Lord of the Rings*, to the west of the Shire, north and south of the Gulf of Lune? The geography of Lindon strongly recalls that of Wales and southwestern England, deeply divided by the Bristol Channel, while the lost land of Beleriand may refer to the lost lands of Lyonesse, off the Cornish coast—in legend swallowed by the ocean in a single night—as well as to the sunken kingdom of Cantre'r Gwaelod, in Wales's Cardigan Bay.

Just like the palimpsest geography of Middle-earth, this simple recipe, made from fresh crabmeat, recalls at once the wild, rocky coastline of Lindon and that of Cornwall and Wales.

⌐—··—⌐

This crab pâté is very versatile: for speedy but impressive canapés, you can serve it on mini blinis—Russian-style pancakes—or for a dinner-party starter, pile it into individual ramekins and serve with whole-wheat toast triangles and lemon wedges to squeeze over.

Serves 4–6
Prep time 10 minutes

30–36 ready-made cocktail-sized blinis
2 cups white crabmeat
½ cup cream cheese
1–2 teaspoons sweet chili sauce, to taste (optional)
2–3 teaspoons lemon juice, to taste
salt and pepper
snipped chives or cilantro, to garnish (optional)

1. Wrap the blinis in foil and warm them in the oven at 350°F, or according to the package instructions.

2. Meanwhile, add the remaining ingredients to a bowl and mash with a fork to the desired consistency. (This can be done in a food processor if you wish.) Season to taste.

3. Serve the pâté with the warmed blinis, garnishing with the chives, if desired.

Elwing's White Pizza

Eärendil's (see page 58) wife is the Half-elven princess Elwing, whose name means "Star-foam" and who was called "the White." Her story strongly recalls the many human–animal metamorphoses found in Greek mythology and seems to have been in part inspired by Ovid's tale of Ceyx and Alcyone in *Metamorphoses*. During her husband's absence at sea, Elwing is left in possession of one of the Silmarils and, to escape the sons of Fëanor who come in search of it, she throws herself off a headland, but is transformed into a great white seabird. In this form, she flies over the ocean to be reunited with her husband. Tolkien does not tell us which type of bird she becomes, but from the description we might imagine a large gull or an albatross, a bird often revered by sailors.

This beautiful pizza, white with mozzarella, is our tribute to this courageous heroine.

———··———

For a super-speedy meal, build your own pizza without the faff, using ready-made pizza crusts. Use this recipe as a template and then get as creative as you like by varying the toppings. Good choices include olives, anchovies, capers, strained tomatoes, chilies, sliced peppers, and mushrooms or ham, blue cheese, and pepperoni.

Serves 4
Prep + cook time 15 minutes

4 ready-made mini pizza crusts

2 garlic cloves, halved

2 cups mozzarella cheese, shredded

5 oz. prosciutto, sliced

1 cup arugula

balsamic vinegar, to taste

salt and pepper

1. Rub the top surfaces of the pizza crusts with the cut faces of the garlic cloves.

2. Put the pizza crusts on a baking sheet, top with the mozzarella, and bake in the oven at 400°F for 10 minutes until the crusts are golden.

3. Top the pizzas with slices of prosciutto and arugula, season to taste with salt and pepper, and a drizzle of balsamic vinegar, and serve straight away.

Fingolfin's Salt Cod Fritters

Fëanor's desire for revenge against Morgoth, who has stolen the Elf-smith's most prized creation, the Silmarils (see pages 25, 61, and 120), leads to the Kinslaying at Alqualondë and the subsequent Flight of the Noldor from Valinor. While Fëanor and his sons steal away in the ships of the Teleri to pursue Morgoth to Middle-earth, his kindred, led by his half-brother Fingolfin, have to make the journey by trekking across the frozen seas in the far north, the Helcaraxë—a journey of great hardship that leads to the death of many, including Fingolfin's wife.

It is hard not to imagine Fingolfin and his people as like the early Vikings exploring and settling the northern reaches of the Atlantic, as far, it seems, as Newfoundland (though their preferred transportation method, of course, was the ship). One of the Vikings' staple foods that they took to sustain them in out-of-the-way places was dried fish—*harðfiskur* in Icelandic—which was preserved by being dried on open-air wooden racks and which could last for several years. Perhaps Fingolfin and his people, too, took their supplies with them and from time to time comforted themselves with a heartening dish like this one before they faced the next stage of their grueling journey into exile and uncertainty.

continued on the following page ⇾

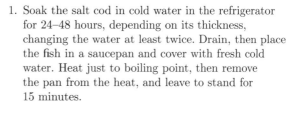

With a crispy coating and fluffy insides with juicy pieces of salt cod, these are delicious served piping hot with aperitifs or as a starter. Serve with lemon wedges for squeezing over and, for an extra-indulgent treat, perhaps a bowl of creamy garlic mayo for dipping.

Serves 4
Prep + cook time 50 minutes, plus soaking and standing

8 oz. piece of salt cod
3 cups potatoes, peeled and quartered
1 shallot, grated
1 egg yolk
1 bunch of parsley, chopped
all-purpose flour, for dusting
vegetable oil, for deep-frying
salt
lemon wedges, to serve

1. Soak the salt cod in cold water in the refrigerator for 24–48 hours, depending on its thickness, changing the water at least twice. Drain, then place the fish in a saucepan and cover with fresh cold water. Heat just to boiling point, then remove the pan from the heat, and leave to stand for 15 minutes.

2. Meanwhile, cook the potatoes in a separate saucepan of lightly salted boiling water for 15 minutes until tender. Drain well, then return to the pan and mash until smooth. Drain the salt cod, discard any skin and bones, then flake into small pieces. Squeeze away any excess water from the shallot. Stir the salt cod, shallot, egg yolk, and parsley into the mashed potato. Using your hands, form the mixture into about 16 small egg shapes, and dust all over with flour.

3. Pour the oil into a large, deep saucepan or deep-fat fryer to a depth of at least 3 inches and heat to 350–375°F, or until a cube of bread browns in 30 seconds. Deep-fry the croquettes in two or three batches for about 3 minutes until golden, then remove with a slotted spoon. Drain on paper towels and keep warm while you cook the remaining croquettes.

4. Serve warm with lemon wedges for squeezing over.

Legolas's Duck in Lettuce Boats

In *The Lord of the Rings*, the Lord of Lothlórien, Celeborn, equips the Fellowship with three Elvish boats to aid their journey south, along the Silverlode (see page 48) and then on down the Great River toward Gondor. Tolkien describes the boats as made out of a gray wood but very light and propelled with short paddles with leaflike blades—and as rather hard to steer, even if remarkably buoyant. It's a description that might make us think of the wicker-and-hide-covered boats of ancient Britain and Ireland—the Irish corrach and Welsh coracle—fragile boats that the early wandering saints of the islands were said to sail in as they went from community to community spreading the word of God.

Our Eastern-inspired dish here uses lettuce-leaf coracles in which to float lightly spiced spoonfuls of duck—a bird that, incidentally, would probably have flourished along the reedy banks of the Anduin, and which the expert marksman Legolas could easily have hunted with his bow. Some of the other ingredients he might have found it harder to come by, though!

The essential ingredient in this sticky and fragrant hot duck salad is Chinese five spice, a warming mix of fennel, clove, star anise, cassia, and ginger. For a more substantial meal, serve the duck over a tangle of egg noodles, perhaps with steamed bok choy on the side.

Serves 4
Prep + cook time 30 minutes

2 tablespoons sesame oil

2 duck breasts, about 6 oz. each, cut into thin strips

2 teaspoons Chinese five spice powder

2 tablespoons dark soy sauce

2 tablespoons clear honey

2 tablespoons toasted sesame seeds

8 Boston lettuce leaves

To garnish
4 scallions, finely chopped

1 small carrot, peeled and grated

1. Heat the oil in a heavy-bottomed skillet. Toss the duck strips with the Chinese five spice powder in a bowl, then fry over high heat for 8–10 minutes until cooked and crispy. Add the soy sauce and honey, and cook for an additional 2 minutes to coat in the sticky glaze. Sprinkle with the sesame seeds and keep warm.

2. Wash and pat dry the lettuce leaves and place on a serving board. Place spoonfuls of the duck into the leaves, then garnish each with the scallions and carrot.

Vingilótë Turnovers

The Half-elven Eärendil—father of Elrond and Elros—is the savior-like figure of the Elves and Men of Beleriand who sails to Valinor to seek the aid of the Valar in their struggle against Morgoth in Middle-earth. He was, in fact, the first figure Tolkien imagined in his evolving mythos—whose origins lie at the outbreak of World War I when Europe was rushing headlong into destruction. In Tolkien's poem relating the story of the voyage of Eärendil, the hero becomes the Evening and Morning Star, a symbol of hope and resurrection.

Eärendil's ship is the *Vingilótë*, which, under Círdan's guidance, he makes out of white beechwood, and rigs with silver sails. Moved by the plight of the Elves and Men, the Valar accept his plea and launch an all-out war on Morgoth. They bless Eärendil's ship and raise it into the air and, with one of the Silmarils displayed on his brow, the Half-elven pilot takes part in the final great battle—the War of Wrath—slaying the dragon Ancalagon. While Eärendil as the Evening Star and Redeemer has clear associations with Christ, who in Revelations is called the Bright and Morning Star, Tolkien may also have been thinking of the Greek star constellation Argo Navis ("the Ship Argo"), which commemorated the magical ship of Jason and the Argonauts.

Our boat-shaped turnovers here commemorate the *Vingilótë*—we might even imagine Eärendil taking one of these delicious treats on board each night as he makes his journey across the skies.

These little pies, packed with colorful vegetables, are delicious served warm or cold with a salad. And they are ideal no-cutlery-needed picnic fare too. For a meaty version, omit the peppers and mix 2 oz. diced ham into the tomato mixture once it has cooled.

Makes 4
Prep + cook time 1 hour

1 tablespoon olive oil

1 onion, chopped

2 garlic cloves, finely chopped

1 zucchini, diced

½ yellow bell pepper, diced

½ red bell pepper, diced

13-oz. can chopped tomatoes

1 tablespoon chopped rosemary or
   basil

½ teaspoon superfine sugar

beaten egg, to glaze

salt and pepper

For the pastry

1 cup bread flour, plus extra
   for dusting

⅓ cup butter, diced

¾ cup mature cheddar cheese, diced,
   plus extra, grated, for sprinkling

2 egg yolks

2 teaspoons water

1. Heat the oil in a saucepan, add the onion, and fry for 5 minutes until softened. Add the garlic, zucchini, and diced peppers and fry briefly, then add the tomatoes, herbs, sugar, and a little salt and pepper. Simmer, uncovered, for 10 minutes, stirring from time to time until thickened. Cool.

2. Make the pastry. Add the flour, butter, and a little salt and pepper to a bowl, rub in the butter with your fingertips until you have fine crumbs, then stir in the cheese. Add the egg yolks and water, and mix to form a smooth dough.

3. Knead lightly on a lightly floured surface, then cut the dough into four pieces. Roll one of the pieces out between two sheets of plastic wrap, patting into a neat shape until you have a 7-inch circle. Remove the top sheet of plastic wrap, spoon a fourth of the filling in the center, brush the pastry edges with beaten egg, then fold the pastry circle in half while still on the lower piece of plastic wrap.

4. Peel the pastry off the wrap, lift onto an oiled cookie sheet, press the edges together well, and press together any breaks in the pastry. Repeat with the remaining pastry pieces and filling until four pies have been made.

5. Brush with beaten egg, sprinkle with a little extra cheese, and bake in the oven at 375°F for 20 minutes until golden brown. Loosen and transfer to a wire rack.

Blue Wizard Steaks

One of the great, unsolved mysteries of Tolkien's legendarium is what becomes of the two blue-robed Istari—wizards—who, unlike Gandalf, Saruman, and Radagast—wander into the east of Middle-earth. In Valinor, the Maia Alatar was in the service of Oromë, as probably was his friend, Pallando, so it may have been perfectly natural for them to explore the eastern regions, the old haunts of their master, the Huntsman himself. Tolkien was somewhat cagey about their fate—hinting that they may have failed, like Saruman, in their mission and became the founder of obscure cults. We prefer to think, however, that they remained faithful, fighting the part of the Free Peoples of Middle-earth at Sauron's back door. They also took care of Oromë's 'sun-cattle" (page 43) and treated themselves to the occasional Kine of Araw steak.

When you're after a quick but delicious lunch, these succulent steaks with their chili-spiked sauce are just the thing. All you need to serve alongside is a crisp green salad, or if you fancy something a bit heartier, some new potatoes or a few fries.

Serves 4
Prep + cook time 20 minutes

2 tablespoons olive oil

4 fillet steaks, about 6 oz. each

2 tablespoons balsamic vinegar

¼ cup full-bodied red wine

4 tablespoons beef stock

2 garlic cloves, chopped

1 teaspoon crushed fennel seeds

1 tablespoon sun-dried tomato paste

½ teaspoon crushed dried chilies

salt and pepper

chopped Italian parsley, to garnish

1. Heat the oil in a nonstick skillet until smoking hot, add the steaks, and cook over very high heat for about 2 minutes on each side, if you want your steaks to be medium rare. For well-done steaks cook for 4–5 minutes on each side. Remove from the pan, season with salt and pepper, and keep warm.

2. Pour the vinegar, wine, and stock into the pan and boil for 30 seconds, scraping any sediment from the base of the pan. Add the garlic and fennel seeds, then whisk in the sun-dried tomato paste and crushed chilies. Bring the sauce to a boil, then boil fast to reduce down until syrupy.

3. Transfer the steaks to serving plates, pouring any collected meat juices into the sauce. Return the sauce to a boil, then season with salt and pepper.

4. Slice the steaks before serving, if desired. Pour the sauce over the steaks and serve immediately, garnished with chopped parsley.

Fëanor's Fiery Pumpkin Bake

Fëanor is one of the lead characters of *The Silmarillion*—a hot-headed, proud Noldorin Elf-prince who is the Elves' greatest craftsman and smith. In type, he is similar to the 'culture heroes' found in many real-world mythologies—like Prometheus in Greek mythology or Coyote in Native American myths—heroes who defy the gods in order to bring new or forbidden technologies into the world. Fëanor creates not only the Silmarils—the transcendently beautiful gems that are the leitmotif of *The Silmarillion*—but also the Tengwar script—of which we find examples in *The Hobbit* and *The Lord of the Rings*.

Like Prometheus, the jewel smith Fëanor is closely associated with fire—even his name means 'Spirit of Fire." His fiery temperament brings disaster to his people, the Noldor, who, because of his pride and embittered desire for revenge, must live in exile in Middle-earth. This oven-baked dish, with its jewel-like colors and mouth-tingling heat, is the perfect commemoration of this gifted but flawed hero of the First Age.

Earthy beet and sweet pumpkin contrast beautifully with the creamy, tangy goat cheese in this one-pan vegetarian dish. It requires hardly any hands-on time so is ideal for a light midweek dinner. The beet will stain your hands, so you may want to wear rubber gloves when peeling and chopping it.

Serves 4
Prep + cook time 50 minutes

3 cups raw beets, peeled and diced

6 cups pumpkin or butternut squash, peeled, deseeded, and cut into slightly larger dice than the beets

1 red onion, cut into wedges

2 tablespoons olive oil

2 teaspoons fennel seeds

½ teaspoon chipotle chili flakes

2 small goat cheeses, 3½ oz. each

salt and pepper

chopped rosemary, to garnish

1. Put the vegetables into a roasting pan, drizzle with the oil, and sprinkle with the fennel seeds, chili flakes, and salt and pepper. Roast in the oven at 400°F for 20–25 minutes, turning once, until well browned and tender.

2. Cut the goat cheeses into thirds and nestle among the roasted vegetables. Sprinkle the cheeses with a little salt and pepper, and drizzle with some of the pan juices.

3. Return the dish to the oven and cook for about 5 minutes until the cheese is just beginning to melt. Sprinkle with rosemary and serve immediately.

Lúthien's Asparagus Pie

The story of the mortal Beren and the Elf-maid Lúthien is one of the central stories of Tolkien's legendarium—a tale told in *The Silmarillion* but also told in brief by Aragorn to Frodo in *The Lord of the Rings*. They are archetypal lovers like Tristan and Isolde or Orpheus and Eurydice, with whose stories theirs has some striking resemblances, and their enduring love, against all the odds—a resistant father, a vengeful dark lord, and even death itself— prefigures that of their descendants Aragorn and Arwen in Tolkien's epic novel.

For Tolkien, Lúthien was also an idealization and commemoration of his own great love, his wife, Edith, who is even called by that name on the Tolkiens' shared gravestone in Wolvercote Cemetery, Oxford, just as the writer is called Beren. In Tolkien's stories, Lúthien is the most beautiful of the Elves and is closely associated with the spring—flowers bloom beneath her feet as she passes and her voice is said to melt away the winter's ice and cold. What better dish, then, to honor Tolkien's heroine than a pie made from asparagus, whose tender green shoots appear all too briefly in the springtime?

———•••———

Serve this delicious asparagus pie hot topped with Parmesan shavings and arugula or—for a pretty-as-a-picture pie—allow to cool and sprinkle with a handful of edible flowers. Look for edible flower mixes, including cornflowers, pansies, and nasturtiums, in the chilled vegetable aisle of big grocery stores.

Serves 2
Prep + cook time 25 minutes

4 oz. asparagus spears, trimmed
6-oz. sheet of ready-rolled
  puff pastry
1 tablespoon ready-made pesto
4 cherry tomatoes, halved

To serve (optional)
Parmesan cheese shavings
arugula
balsamic glaze
edible flowers

1. Cook the asparagus in a saucepan of lightly salted boiling water for 2 minutes. Drain and rinse under cold water, then drain again.

2. Place the pastry on a cookie sheet. Spread the pesto evenly over the pastry, leaving a ½-inch border around the edge. Arrange the asparagus on the pesto. Place the tomatoes on top.

3. Bake in the oven at 400°F for 15–20 minutes until the pastry is crisp and golden. Serve warm with Parmesan cheese shavings, arugula, and a drizzle of balsamic syrup, or at room temperature, sprinkled with edible flowers.

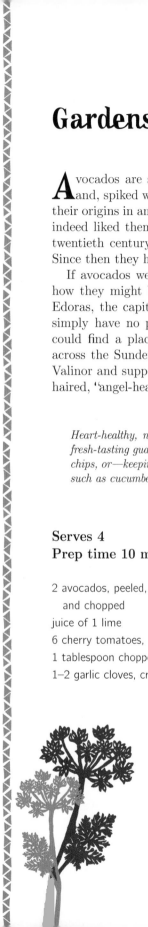

Gardens of Lórien Avocado

Avocados are so commonplace today—served on sourdough for breakfast and, spiked with cilantro and chili, as guacamole—that it is easy to forget their origins in ancient Mesoamerica. European conquistadors first tasted, and indeed liked them in the sixteenth century, but it would only be in the late twentieth century that they reached European stores in any great quantity. Since then they have become every hipster's superfood.

If avocados were met with wonder and mirth in 1970s suburbia, imagine how they might be viewed in Third Age Gondorian Minas Tirith, let alone Edoras, the capital of Rohan, built in the wooden Anglo-Saxon style. They simply have no place in the cuisines of Middle-earth. Perhaps, though, we could find a place for them in Aman, Tolkien's America-like continent, far across the Sundering Seas—luxuriantly growing in the Gardens of Lórien in Valinor and supped upon by those highest of High Elves, the Vanya—golden-haired, "angel-headed hipsters" if ever there were.

Heart-healthy, nutrient-dense avocado is the star of the show in this simple, fresh-tasting guacamole recipe. Serve with strips of toasted pita bread or tortilla chips, or—keeping with the healthy theme—with oatcakes and vegetable crudités, such as cucumber, peppers, and carrots.

Serves 4
Prep time 10 minutes

2 avocados, peeled, pitted,
 and chopped
juice of 1 lime
6 cherry tomatoes, diced
1 tablespoon chopped cilantro leaves
1–2 garlic cloves, crushed

1. Put the avocados and lime juice in a bowl, and mash together to prevent discoloration, then stir in the remaining ingredients.

2. Serve immediately.

Dining in Valinor

Tolkien's classification of the Elves is highly complex—in part reflecting the strong sense of identity that his Elves themselves possessed. Not only do they seem to have a fierce pride regarding their kindred—Teleri, Noldor or Vanyar—but they were also sharply aware of the decisive division between those who have been to Aman ("the blessed realm") and seen the light of the Two Trees—the Caliquendi ("Elves of the Light")—and those who have not—the Moriquendi ("Elves of Darkness") either because they refuse outright to heed the summons of the Valar (the Avari) or because, for various reasons, they turn aside from the journey—the Úmanyar ("those not of Aman").

On Tolkien's Arda, Aman was originally a continent situated to the west of Middle-earth, across the great sea Belegaer. Although it is the home of the immortal Valar and Maiar—Tolkien's greater and lesser powers—and many of the likewise immortal Elves, and is hence known as the Undying Lands, it is a "real," physical place, with its own geography, flora, and fauna, just like Middle-earth. At the end of the Second Age, after the downfall of Númenor, and the catastrophic Changing of Arda from flat to spherical, the continent of Aman is removed from the world altogether, reachable only by the Elves (and a few others) by sailing along the Straight Road, half on the sea, half in the sky.

By this cosmological account, Aman cannot be the Americas—which in any case physically differ from the continent of the Valar. Nonetheless, Tolkien's conception of Aman was undoubtedly influenced by the Americas, which in the first centuries after their "discovery" by Europeans in 1492 were described in terms of an earthly paradise, as a promised land of peace and plenty. Tolkien's descriptions of Valinor—the land of the Valar in Aman—with the Two Trees stretching toward heaven and the Eden-like Gardens of Lórien—may remind us of Christopher Columbus's hyperbolic description (1493) of the island of Hispaniola with its "most lofty mountains [. . .] all most beautiful in a thousand shapes, and all accessible, and full of trees of a thousand kinds, [where] the nightingale was singing, and other birds of a thousand sorts." This description, and many others like it in later decades, struck a chord in a Europe torn by war and want, helping to fuel wave after wave of immigration and colonial

settlement. In Tolkien's legendarium, Aman has a similar resonance as a 'land of milk and honey" among the peoples of Middle-earth, especially, of course, the Elves, who feel an unceasing urge to sail west across the sea to the utopia of their hearts.

So far, and throughout the rest of this book, then, we have imagined an Aman that is both like and unlike America, offering foodstuffs that, strictly speaking, are impossible in Middle-earth but conceivable in Aman; all the New World produce that we take for granted today— potatoes, tomatoes, avocados, blueberries, pumpkins, and so on. (Tolkien took similar liberties with the logic of his world, allowing both the potato and tobacco plant to feature prominently in his Middle-earth, 'Old World" flora, so we feel no qualms!) On this basis we have evolved something of an Amanian cuisine, imagining the food and drink of the Elves of Aman, and even, on occasion, dining with the Valar themselves.

Main Dishes

Everyone is for ever hungry in *The Hobbit*—whether they're the title character, a Dwarf, a wizard, a spider, a goblin, a dragon . . . or even an Elf. The characters and the monsters they meet all seem to have food on the brain and are always wondering about their next meal. In part, this is because *The Hobbit* is a children's book—kids love reading about food (though, to be honest, don't we all?), and partly because Bilbo Baggins—true to Hobbit-kind—is so heavily invested in food, and it's his point of view that we are following in the story. In his Hobbit-centric eyes, everyone just has to be thinking of their stomachs.

Nonetheless, we may be a little shocked that the Elves, too, have healthy appetites, especially if we come to *The Hobbit* with certain prejudices nurtured by *The Lord of the Rings* or, especially, by *The Silmarillion*. Aren't they just too ethereal and, well, too fey to have anything so base as an appetite? Yet here in *The Hobbit* we find them, again and again, feasting, guzzling, and, what's more, talking and singing about food . . . and not any old food, but proper, stomach-lining, heavy-duty food—meatballs and bannocks, and rich red wine.

In this section, then, you will find dishes, hearty ones as well as more refined ones, that might especially satisfy the Elves as Tolkien portrayed them in *The Hobbit*. We don't imagine, though, that the Elves of Beleriand or Lothlórien would turn their nose up at them either.

Eregion Root Vegetable Stew

We have named this tasty, comforting stew for the Noldor kingdom of Eregion, which lies just to the west of the Misty Mountains and the Dwarvish realm of Moria. It is here that, during the Second Age, Sauron tricks the Elven jewel smiths—the Gwaith-i-Mírdain, led by Celebrimbor, grandson of Fëanor (page 61)—into forging the Rings of Power (page 79). In *The Lord of the Rings* the Fellowship pass through the region, but it has been destroyed many hundreds of years before—one of the many ruined or wasted kingdoms, Elven, Dwarven, and Dúnedain, which haunt Tolkien's Middle-earth. It is almost as if he is conjuring up 'Dark Age" Britain—its hills scattered with the melancholy ruins of its Roman past.

While in Eregion, the Fellowship may well have eaten this stew, made from gathered roots, while sitting under the ruins of Celebrimbor's guild-house where, long before, the Rings of Power were made.

⌐━━•••━━⌐

Comfort in a steaming bowl, this is what you'll want to eat after a brisk walk on a cold day. It freezes well, so you can double up the quantities and make a big batch.

Serves 4
Prep + cook time 1½ hours

½ cup pearl barley

2 tablespoons olive oil

1 large onion, finely chopped

2 leeks, trimmed, cleaned, and finely chopped

1 celery stick, finely chopped

1½ lb. mixed root vegetables, such as parsnips, rutabaga, turnips, carrots, and potatoes, evenly diced

4 cups vegetable stock

1 bouquet garni

salt and pepper

1. Bring a large saucepan of water to a boil and pour in the pearl barley. Cook at a gentle simmer for 30 minutes. Drain well.

2. Meanwhile, heat the oil in a large, heavy-bottomed saucepan over medium-low heat, add the onion, leeks, and celery, and fry gently for 8–10 minutes, or until softened but not colored. Add the root vegetables and cook for an additional 5 minutes, stirring regularly.

3. Pour in the stock, add the bouquet garni, and bring to a boil. Stir in the pearl barley, then reduce the heat and simmer for 25–30 minutes, or until the vegetables and pearl barley are tender. Remove the bouquet garni and season to taste with salt and pepper. Ladle into bowls and serve.

Vanyar Cannellini Bean Stew

Tolkien depicts Valinor—part New World, part paradise—as a land of plenty. Its characteristic landscape is the garden, nature perfected and preened—as exemplified by the Gardens of Lórien, somewhere to the south of the land. Lórien appears to be largely ornamental—with flowers and trees grown, above all, for their soothing beauty—though we can imagine that the Vanyar—the 'Fair Elves" who live in Valinor—kept practical kitchen gardens, too. As New World Elves, we might think of them as something like Mesoamerican peoples who for hundreds of years before the European conquest tilled the land to produce the classic trio of crops—the 'three sisters" of corn, squash, and beans.

It takes a lot of work to tend to a paradise, and this quick-and-easy bean stew would have been a welcome dish for any Vanyar, king or subject, after a hard day's work in the garden.

* * *

This vegan bean stew is a real winter warmer and very budget-friendly. You can vary the beans, depending on what's in your pantry—cranberry beans and lima beans work especially well. Serve with crusty bread or over baked potatoes.

Serves 4
Prep + cook time 30 minutes

3 tablespoons olive oil

1 small onion, chopped

2 garlic cloves, finely chopped

2 carrots, peeled and diced

1 tablespoon rosemary, leaves picked and chopped

2 x 13-oz. cans cannellini beans, rinsed and drained

2 cups vegetable stock

salt and pepper

1. Heat the olive oil in a large, heavy-bottomed skillet and cook the onion, garlic, carrots, and rosemary over medium heat, stirring occasionally, for 3–4 minutes until softened.

2. Add the cannellini beans and vegetable stock, and bring to a boil. Simmer briskly, uncovered, for 10 minutes until piping hot, then carefully scoop out a third of the beans.

3. Place in a food processor and blitz until smooth. Return the pureed beans to the pan, stir to combine, and heat through. Season to taste, then serve.

Moriquendi Bean and Lentil Curry

The Noldor seem to use the term "Moriquendi" as an insult to the Avari, perhaps because they refuse outright to heed the summons of the Valar (page 66). Most of the Avari freely return their hostility. Tolkien nowhere suggests that the Avari are evil, though in the early days some were captured, corrupted, and bred to become the race of Orcs, who undoubtedly are.

This striking dish of black lentils and beans is our tribute to the Dark Elves—that forgotten, secretive people—its black colors and Eastern flavors evoking the dark forests of the far east of Middle-earth.

———— ··· ————

This black-eyed pea dish really delivers both on flavor and health benefits. It's full of zingy spices and provides plenty of fiber, protein, iron, vitamins, and antioxidants. Don't forget to start the prepping the evening before by soaking the lentils.

Serves 4
Prep + cook time 1½ hours, plus soaking

⅔ cup dried split black lentils, rinsed and drained

2 cups boiling water

1 tablespoon peanut oil

1 onion, finely chopped

3 garlic cloves, crushed

2 teaspoons peeled and finely grated fresh ginger

2 fresh green chilies, halved lengthwise

1 teaspoon each of ground turmeric, paprika, cumin, and coriander

13-oz. can black-eyed peas, rinsed and drained

2 cups cold water

3 cups baby spinach

large handful of chopped cilantro leaves

salt

1 cup fat-free plain yogurt, whisked, to serve

1. Place the lentils in a deep bowl and cover with cold water. Leave to soak for 10–12 hours. Transfer to a colander and rinse under cold running water. Drain and place in a medium saucepan with the measured boiling water. Bring to a boil, then reduce the heat to low.

2. Simmer gently for 35–40 minutes, skimming off any scum that rises to the surface and stirring often.

3. Heat the oil in a large saucepan and add the onion, garlic, ginger, and chilies. Stir-fry for 5–6 minutes and then add the turmeric, paprika, cumin, ground coriander, black-eyed peas, and lentils.

4. Add the measured cold water and bring to a boil. Reduce the heat and stir in the spinach. Cook gently for 10–15 minutes, stirring often. Remove from the heat and season with salt to taste. Stir in the chopped cilantro and drizzle with the yogurt. Sprinkle with a little paprika and serve immediately.

Gil-galad Golden Dhal

Part of the extraordinary achievement and wonder of Tolkien's Middle-earth is that not only did he create its epic present—the late Third Age as presented in the novels *The Hobbit* and *The Lord of the Rings*—but also its mythological history and hinterland, a distant heroic age—the First and Second Ages—as found in *The Silmarillion* and elsewhere. This gives his work a sense of grandeur and depth that makes it comparable with the great 'national' epics that so inspired him—from Homer's *Iliad* to the Anglo-Saxon *Beowulf*, which similarly look back to a golden age of larger-than-life heroes.

Looming large in the pantheon of the Second Age is Gil-galad—'Star of Radiance'—the last High King of the Elves who defeats Sauron but is himself slain in their struggle. In the Third Age he remains a figure of hope and resilience, and appears in *The Lord of the Rings* as a mythic hero, the subject of song and tale—most notably when Sam recalls the opening verses of a heroic song about him, as taught to him by Bilbo as a boy: 'Gil-galad was an elven-king . . .'

The golden color of this dish is symbolic of the golden memory of this last great Elven king, as he rides with his troops against Sauron, shields and banners raised high.

───── ·· ─────

This works as a vegan main course for a couple of people—spoon over some thick dairy-free yogurt with a little spicy harissa paste stirred through, and serve with toasted flatbreads alongside—or as side dish for grilled or roasted meat and poultry.

Serves 2
Prep + cook time 45 minutes

2 tablespoons olive oil

2 onions, finely chopped

4 garlic cloves, finely chopped

2 teaspoons ground turmeric

2 teaspoons ground fenugreek

1 cup dried yellow lentils, rinsed and
   drained

13-oz. can chopped tomatoes

2 teaspoons sugar

2½ cups water

small bunch of cilantro, finely chopped

salt and pepper

1. Heat the oil in the base of a large, heavy-bottomed saucepan over medium heat, stir in the onions and garlic, and cook for 2–3 minutes to soften a little. Add the turmeric, fenugreek, and lentils, stir to coat well, then stir in the tomatoes and sugar.

2. Pour in the measured water and bring to a boil, then reduce the heat, cover, and cook gently for about 30 minutes until the lentils are tender but not mushy, adding a little more water if necessary. Stir in half the chopped cilantro and season with salt and pepper. Serve garnished with the remaining cilantro.

Cuiviénen Mussels

The Awakening of the Elves takes place in the far east of Middle-earth, in the forests around the Bay of Cuiviénen, part of the Inland Sea of Helcar. The event is briefly described in *The Silmarillion*, but was also the subject of a late, somewhat curious work of Tolkien's known as ''The Cuivienyarna.'' This is essentially what purports to be a piece of archaic Elven lore describing the exponential increase in the number of Elves after the initial awakening of pairs of Elves, prosaically named in Quena ''First,'' ''Second,'' and ''Third''—the forebears of the Vanyar, Noldor, and Teleri.

Over time the Elves learn by a process of trial and error the rudiments of culture—language, poetry, and song, certainly; shelter and clothing; and fire for warmth and, no doubt, cooking. Perhaps, as these childlike Elves wandered on the seashore of Helcar looking in wonder at the new world they found themselves in, they gathered mussels from the rocks. Later they may have cooked them simply with herbs, rather as in this recipe, though wine, admittedly, was probably still some way away along the Elves' evolutionary path.

⌒—···—⌒

Food doesn't have to be complicated; sometimes a simple one-pot meal is just right—this French classic is a great example. Serve with fresh crusty bread to mop up every last drop of the wine and garlic-scented cooking juices.

Serves 4
Prep + cook time 15 minutes

2 tablespoons olive oil
2 garlic cloves, sliced
3 lb. live mussels, scrubbed and
   debearded
⅔ cup dry white wine
handful of Italian parsley, chopped

1. Heat the oil in a large saucepan. Add the garlic and cook for 30 seconds until lightly golden. Add the mussels, discarding any that are cracked or don't shut when tapped, and the wine.

2. Cover the pan and cook for 5 minutes, shaking the pan occasionally, or until the mussels have opened. Discard any that remain closed.

3. Stir in the parsley and serve immediately.

Isle of Balar Grilled Lobster

In the First Age, the Isle of Balar lies to the south of Beleriand, in the Bay of Balar, Christopher Tolkien's map of Beleriand showing it as a leaflike island with low-lying mountains at its southern tip. According to the tales of the Elves, it was a fragment of Tol Eressëa, the floating island that Ulmo used to bring the Eldar to Aman (page 45). During the Wars of Beleriand, it becomes a refuge for Elves escaping the devastation—both Noldor from Gondolin (page 31) and the Falathrim of Círdan (page 21). It also becomes home to havens from which the Elves send out ships to seek the aid of the Valar, including Eärendil's Vingilot.

The refugees no doubt depended on the sea to feed themselves. The coastal-dwelling Falathrim would have been very used to the diet on offer, but the rather spoiled Elves of Gondolin much less so. Perhaps the delicious lobster dish here would have tempted the Noldor to try something new, though.

⸺ ··⸺

This stunning-looking dish is surprisingly easy to make and a luxurious choice for a special occasion. Serve with a green salad dressed with a sharp lemony vinaigrette to cut through the rich flavors, and perhaps some crusty bread for soaking up the creamy sauce.

Serves 4
Prep + cook time 25 minutes

½ cup butter, softened
1 garlic clove, crushed
1 tablespoon lemon juice
large handful of chopped parsley
large handful of chopped chives
2 cooked lobsters
salt and pepper

To serve
green salad with fennel
potato wedges

1. Mix together the butter, garlic, lemon juice, and herbs and season with salt and pepper. Place in a sheet of plastic wrap, roll into a cylinder, and twist the ends to seal. Put in the freezer for 5 minutes to harden a little.

2. Snap the claws away from the lobsters and crack the shell with the back of a heavy knife to remove the meat inside.

3. Cut each lobster body in half lengthwise. Wash out the head cavities with cold water and divide the claw meat between them.

4. Put the lobsters on a broiler pan, cut side up, slice the butter, and place on top. Cook under a hot broiler for 5–7 minutes until bubbling. Serve with green salad and potato wedges.

Lauterbrunnen Trout

One of the inspirations for Rivendell—the refuge of the Elves nestled in a secret valley in the foothills of the Misty Mountains—is the Lauterbrunnental in Switzerland, an idyllic 'trough," or steep-sided, alpine valley in the canton of Bern famous for its springs and waterfalls. Tolkien went hiking in the valley as a young man in 1911 and painted watercolors that would later evolve into his depictions—both literary and artistic—of Elrond's green, hidden valley. The name of the river that flows through Rivendell, the Bruinen, or the Loudwater, plays on the Swiss valley's name, which itself seems to mean either 'Many Springs" or 'Loud Springs."

The streams of the Lauterbrunnental teem with trout—the inspiration for this fresh-tasting dish.

A go-to recipe when you need dinner in a dash, this elegant trout dish is wonderful with some buttered new potatoes and asparagus in spring, or with a fresh green salad in summer. And it looks impressive too!

Serves 4–6
Prep + cook time 30 minutes

3 tablespoons olive oil
3 lb. piece of trout, cut into 2 fillets
1 lemon, sliced
handful of mixed herbs, finely chopped
salt

For the tartare
6 tablespoons mayonnaise
2 teaspoons drained capers, roughly
    chopped
1 scallion, chopped
1 teaspoon superfine sugar
1 teaspoon whole-grain mustard
lemon juice, to taste
handful of dill, chopped

1. Brush a large baking sheet with a little of the oil. Place one trout fillet, skin-side down, on the prepared sheet, and season with a little salt. Top with the lemon slices and herbs. Season the other fillet and place on top, skin-side up.

2. Tie pieces of kitchen string around the trout to secure. Drizzle over the remaining oil. Cook in the oven at 425°F for 25 minutes, or until just cooked through.

3. Meanwhile, mix together the tartare ingredients and place in a serving bowl. Serve the fish with the tartare alongside.

Stuffed Bream with Samphire

At the end of the First Age, most of the Elvish lands of Beleriand are destroyed and submerged by the sea, leaving just the area known as Lindon beside the Grey Mountains. Some of the hills survive as small islands off Lindon's coast in the Great Sea Belegaer, including Himling, or Himring, on which once stood the fortress of Maedhros, eldest son of Fëanor.

These islands must have been sad enough places, reminders of long-lost realms and heroes. Perhaps sometimes, in the Second Age, Elves and Númenórean Men disembarked on these Western Isles to mull upon their ancient past and kindred. Perhaps, too, they sometimes tarried on the seashores, fishing and gathering samphire from the shingle, so as to make a fine supper for themselves as they watched the sun set down over the Belegaer.

⁘

Samphire is a sea vegetable that grows along the shoreline and in marshes. You can find it at fishmongers and bigger grocery stores. Crunchy and salty, it's the ideal partner for fish, and works really well with the satisfyingly meaty texture of these stuffed bream fillets.

Serves 4
Prep + cook time 1 hour 20 minutes

6 cups russet or other starchy potatoes, thinly sliced
6 tablespoons olive oil
1 tablespoon chopped thyme
4 bream fillets, about 5 oz. each
3 oz. prosciutto, chopped
2 shallots, finely chopped
finely grated rind of 1 lemon
1½ cups samphire
salt and pepper

1. Toss the potato slices with 4 tablespoons of the oil, a little salt and pepper, and the thyme in a bowl. Tip into a roasting pan or ovenproof dish and spread out in an even layer. Cover with foil and bake in the oven at 375°F for about 30 minutes until the potatoes are tender.

2. Score the bream fillets with a sharp knife. Mix the prosciutto with the shallots, lemon rind, and a little pepper, and use to sandwich the bream fillets together. Tie at intervals with string. Cut each of the sandwiched fillets through the center to make four even-sized portions.

3. Lay the fish over the potatoes and return to the oven, uncovered, for an additional 20 minutes, or until the fish is cooked through.

4. Sprinkle the samphire around the fish and drizzle with the remaining oil. Return to the oven for an additional 5 minutes before serving.

The Three Rings

The "golden age" of the Elves is the Age of the Stars and, despite the wars and eventual ruin of Beleriand, the First Age, when Elvish culture and civilization are at their height. Subsequent ages in Middle-earth see the dispersal of the Elves across the west of the continent, the diminishment of Elvish power, and the departure of many of the Elves across the sea to Aman. Through these ages the Elves are acutely conscious that, as a people, they are waning and that their 'time' is drawing to a close, even as the 'dominion' of Men is correspondingly rising. It is in this context, Tolkien suggests, that we should see the forging of the Three Rings—Vilya, Narya, and Nenya—by Celebrimbor in the Second Age—as an ultimately doomed attempt to enable the leaders of the Elves to artificially preserve and sustain Elvish power and beauty.

In the following three recipes we have matched the Three Rings with three curries, each of whose vivid flavors captures something of the ring's character. They might be just the inspiration you need as you and your fellow diners conspire to combine your powers to overthrow the Dark Lord and destroy the influence of the One Ring.

Nenya : Cod and Coconut Curry

The preserving power of the Three Rings is best seen in the Nenya, the Ring of Water, with its adamant (diamond) set into a band of the silverlike mithril. This is wielded by Galadriel, who uses it to encircle the woodland realm of Lothlórien, which in some sense is removed from time and exists in a state of perpetual flourishing. With the destruction of the One Ring, Nenya loses its power and Lothlórien slowly withers. Here the silver-white of Galadriel's ring is expressed in this vibrant creamy curry, whose whiteness is heightened by the forest green of the lime and coriander leaves.

From tying on your apron to putting on the table in under half an hour, this recipe will be a go-to when you need a midweek meal that is speedy and delicious. All it needs is some basmati or brown rice to go alongside. You can replace the cod with any firm white fish.

Serves 4
Prep + cook time 20 minutes

1 tablespoon peanut oil
2 teaspoons ground cumin
2 teaspoons ground coriander
2 green chilies, deseeded and sliced
1 cinnamon stick
1 star anise
6 makrut lime leaves
14-oz. can coconut milk
4 skinless cod loins, about 5 oz. each
juice of 1 lime
fresh cilantro leaves, to garnish
 (optional)

1. Heat the oil in a saucepan, add the spices and lime leaves, and cook, stirring, for 2 minutes until fragrant. Pour in the coconut milk and simmer for 5 minutes.

2. Add the fish and simmer for 4–6 minutes until the fish is tender and cooked through. Stir in the lime juice.

3. Sprinkle with cilantro leaves, if desired.

Narya : Red Curry

The Red Ring, set with a ruby, is the Ring of Fire. Originally Celebrimbor entrusts the ring to Círdan the Shipwright, but he later relinquishes it to Gandalf to help him in his mission in Middle-earth. Like its companion rings, its chief power is to sustain and preserve, but Círdan, in handing it to Galdalf, also suggests that has the power to inspire resistance and resilience in the face of tyranny. The ring's association with fire seems an appropriate one for a wizard associated with fireworks, dragons and, ultimately, his combat with a Balrog, or fire-demon. This Thai curry is inspired by the fiery elements of this ring.

Get dinner on the table in half an hour with this speedy one-pan curry that really delivers on exotic Thai flavors. The creamy coconut milk tames the heat of the curry paste and adds depth and balance. All it needs is some freshly cooked jasmine or white rice.

Serves 4
Prep + cook time 35 minutes

1 tablespoon peanut oil
2–3 tablespoons Thai red curry paste
1 teaspoon ground turmeric
¼ teaspoon ground allspice
1 lb. lean beef, thinly sliced
14-oz. can coconut milk
¾ cup beef stock
3 tablespoons Thai fish sauce
¼ cup palm sugar or brown sugar
4–5 tablespoons tamarind paste
salt and pepper

To garnish
½ red bell pepper, cut into thin strips
2 scallions, shredded

1. Heat the oil in a saucepan and stir-fry the curry paste, turmeric, and allspice over medium heat for 3–4 minutes, or until fragrant.

2. Add the beef and stir-fry for 4–5 minutes. Add the coconut milk, stock, fish sauce, sugar, and tamarind. Reduce the heat and simmer for 10–15 minutes, or until the beef is tender. Season to taste and add a little stock or water if the sauce is too dry.

3. Spoon into bowls, garnish with strips of red pepper and scallion, and serve with rice.

Vilya : Pilaf Rice

The Blue Ring, a sapphire set in a gold band, initially belongs to Gil-galad, the High King of the Elves through the Second Age, but eventually passes into the hands of Elrond. Like Galadriel, we can assume that Elrond uses the ring's power—it is the greatest of the three—to preserve and protect the realm of Rivendell. The golden pilaf here is reminiscent not only of the gold of the ring but the beauty of Rivendell, as captured, likewise, in Tolkien's luminous watercolors of the Hidden Valley.

For a vegan-friendly, health-boosted meal, there's no need to look further than this delicious rice and lentil combination. If you like things a little sweeter, you could stir through a handful of currants or sultanas before serving.

Serves 4
Prep + cook time 40 minutes, plus standing

1 tablespoon peanut oil

1 onion, finely chopped

1 teaspoon ground turmeric

1 tablespoon cumin seeds

1 dried red chili

1 cinnamon stick

3 cloves

½ teaspoon cardamom seeds, crushed

1 cup basmati rice, rinsed

1 cup dried red lentils, rinsed

2 cups vegetable stock

6 tablespoons finely chopped cilantro
  leaves

salt

1. Heat the oil in a large saucepan over medium heat. Add the onion, stir-fry for 6–8 minutes until very soft, then add the spices. Continue to stir-fry for 2–3 minutes until fragrant. Now add the rice and lentils, and stir-fry for an additional 2–3 minutes.

2. Add the stock and cilantro, season to taste, and bring to a boil. Reduce the heat to low, cover the pan, and cook gently for 10–12 minutes, or until all the liquid has been absorbed. Remove from the heat and allow to stand, covered and undisturbed, for 10–15 minutes. Fluff up the grains with a fork and serve.

Greenwood Pheasant with Blackberries

Here is another dish popular, we think, in the Elvenking's halls, served as a simple dinner in the fall when there are plenty of brambles to be raided along the secret Elven paths that crisscross Greenwood the Great. While we scarcely come across Elven children in Tolkien's stories, they are nonetheless carefully described in Tolkien's essay 'Of the marriage laws and customs of the Eldar. . ." They appear, he tells us, much as human children, but much slower to grow and age and long retaining a sense of joy and wonder, 'lingering in the first spring of childhood" and not reaching maturity until 100 years of age. It would be nice to think of blackberrying, then, as the Elven children's business—the pastime of an idyllic and slow-passing youth spent close to nature.

⸻ ··· ⸻

Meaty game and blackberries have a natural affinity, which is why this simple and speedy dish works so well. Serve with the creamy mashed potatoes and steamed kale or cabbage to cut through the sweetness of that heavenly sauce.

Serves 4
Prep + cook time 25 minutes

1 tablespoon butter
1 pheasant, divided into 2 legs and
  2 breasts
½ cup blackberries
5 tablespoons redcurrant jelly
salt and pepper

1. Heat the butter in a skillet over medium heat. Season the pheasant pieces and add to the pan, cooking for 4–5 minutes on each side until golden brown and cooked through. You may need to cook the leg pieces for a little longer. You will know when the meat is done when the juices run clear when you insert a knife into the thickest part of the meat.

2. Add the blackberries and redcurrant jelly and stir until the jelly has melted. Serve immediately with the blackberry sauce spooned over the top.

Nargothrond Chicken

Tolkien's Elves do not only live in forest dwellings and harbor towns, close to the sky, but, like the Dwarves, also in underground cities, delved deep into the sides of hills and river valleys. In this, perhaps, Tolkien was alluding to the Dark Elves of Norse mythology, who dwell deep under the earth. The kindred of Elves known as the Noldor, in particular, are associated with smithery and jewel-making, thus aligning them more closely still with the Dwarves.

We may well wonder what the Elves of this underground realm dined on— no doubt fish from the river Narog, into whose steep banks it is built, together with hunted and gathered foods from the surrounding forests. Perhaps, though, one of the fortress's caves was set aside for raising chickens: here we've imagined a spiced chicken dish served with a bean salad whose bright colors are every bit as bright as Nargothrond's jewels.

—···—

This sweet and sticky chicken packs a tasty punch and is a great midweek meal that uses up the ingredients lurking at the back of your pantry.

Serves 4
Prep + cook time 1 hour 10 minutes

8 chicken thighs or drumsticks
1 teaspoon each cumin seeds, fennel
   seeds, and dried thyme leaves
¼ teaspoon ground cinnamon
½ teaspoon smoked paprika
1 tablespoon each sunflower oil,
   tomato paste, and vinegar
2 tablespoons dark brown sugar
2 tablespoons pineapple juice

Bean salad
7½-oz. can chopped pineapple, juice
   reserved
13-oz. can black-eyed peas
small bunch of cilantro, chopped
½ red onion, finely chopped
1 red bell pepper, diced
grated rind and juice of 1 lime

1. Slash the chicken joints two or three times with a knife, then place in a roasting pan. Roughly crush the seeds, then mix together with the remaining ingredients, and spoon over the chicken.

2. Add 4 tablespoons of water to the base of the roasting pan, then cook in the oven at 350°F for 40 minutes, spooning the pan juices over occasionally until the chicken is deep brown and the juices run clear when the chicken is pierced with a sharp knife.

3. Meanwhile, make the bean salad. Pour the remaining canned pineapple juice into a bowl, then add the chopped pineapple and all the remaining ingredients. Mix together, then serve spoonfuls with the cooked chicken.

Avari Venison Tagine

Tolkien's stories take place largely in the northwest of Middle-earth. While both the Elves and Men originated in the far east of this vast continent before migrating slowly westward, both the east and the south are only very vaguely described. Indeed, many of Tolkien's toponyms for such regions are simply named after the compass points—Harad means 'South' in Sindarin, and Rhûn, 'East.' They are literally little more than empty white spaces on the map, even though Tolkien implies that they are quite heavily populated, mostly by Men, vassals of Sauron.

And yet there must have been many Avari—the 'unwilling' Elves (page 72)—who lived in the east—a secretive people who lived in the region's vast forests and among its hills and who, though they could never acquire the knowledge and skill of their sundered kinsfolk, the Eldar, nonetheless excelled as singers, hunters, weavers, and potters. This might be one of their dishes—brimming with eastern spices and sweet with dried fruits.

⌐—··—⌐

The sweetly spiced fall dish is a great make-ahead choice. Serve it with your favorite side—couscous, brown rice, and quinoa are all good with this—and a dollop of thick yogurt. If you want to ring the changes, replace the venison with shoulder of lamb, and reduce the cooking time to 45 minutes.

Serves 4
Prep + cook time 2¼ hours

1½ lb. venison, cut into cubes
1 onion, chopped
1 garlic clove, crushed
1 teaspoon ground cumin
1 teaspoon ground cinnamon
½ teaspoon ground ginger
1 teaspoon ground turmeric
2 cups chicken stock
2 tablespoons tomato paste
1 teaspoon dark brown sugar
⅔ cup dried apricots
⅔ cup prunes
⅔ cup slivered almonds, toasted

1. Heat the oil in a large saucepan over medium heat and brown the meat (you may have to do this in batches), then remove with a slotted spoon and set aside.

2. Add the onion and garlic to the pan and cook for 2–3 minutes, then stir in the spices and cook for an additional minute.

3. Return the meat to the pan with the stock, tomato paste, and sugar. Bring to a boil, then simmer with the lid on for 1½ hours. Remove the lid, add the dried fruit, and leave to bubble gently for 30 minutes, or until the meat is tender.

4. Serve sprinkled with toasted slivered almonds.

Celegorm's Venison Steaks

Tolkien's portrayal of the Elves, in particular of the Noldor, in part draws on the real-world medieval aristocratic elite as shown in epics and romances such as the *Nibelungenlied* or Wolfram von Eschenbach's *Parzifal*. They are first of all warriors but they also engage in pursuits typical of medieval lords and ladies—they feast, they sing, they recite poetry, and, above all, they hunt.

The greatest of the Noldor huntsmen is Celegorm, the third son of Fëanor (page 61), who while in Valinor is a friend of Oromë (page 89), the Huntsman of the Valar (page 66), and receives from him the giant wolfhound Huan as his hunting companion. In Beleriand, with his brother Curufin, he becomes King of Himlad, and hunts its forests and moors for deer and wild boar. Perhaps these venison steaks were served in the brothers' feasting hall on their return from the hunt, when songs are sung and music played, and Huan sits at his master's feet.

⌐━━··━━⌐

Resting the pepper-and-juniper-crusted venison loin after cooking to allow the juices to creep back in is the key to great results, so resist the urge to cut into it right away. Serve the steaks with green beans, redcurrant jelly, and fries or boiled potatoes.

Serves 4
Prep + cook time 40–55 minutes

1½ lb. loin of venison,
   cut from the haunch
¾ cup mixed peppercorns, crushed
2 tablespoons juniper berries, crushed
1 egg white, lightly beaten
salt

1. Make sure that the venison fits into your broiler pan; if necessary, cut the loin in half to fit.

2. Mix together the peppercorns, juniper berries, and some salt in a large, shallow dish. Dip the venison in the egg white, then roll it in the peppercorn mixture, covering it evenly all over.

3. Cook the venison under a hot broiler for 4 minutes on each of the four sides, turning it carefully so that the crust stays intact. Transfer the loin to a lightly greased roasting pan and cook in the oven at 400°F for an additional 15 minutes for rare, or up to 30 minutes for well done (the time will depend on the thickness of the loin).

4. Leave the venison to rest for a few minutes, then slice it thickly, and serve.

Oromë's Venison Pie

Of all Tolkien's Valar, Oromë the Huntsman and Lord of Forests is perhaps the closest to the Eldar. It is he who first discovers the Firstborn while hunting the creatures of Morgoth under the stars in the far east of Middle-earth and helps guide them on their Great Journey into the West. In the creation of this Vala, Tolkien was inspired by an amalgam of figures from real-world mythology and folklore: among them are the Norse god Heimdall, who possesses the resounding hunting horn Gjallarhorn just as Oromë has the horn Valaroma; the Greek mythological huntsman Orion; and the supernatural Wild Huntsmen of European folk tales, such as the English Herne, who ride through the night punishing the wicked.

Although Oromë is indefatigable in hunting down the creatures of Morgoth, we can easily imagine him in a gentler guise, settling down to eat with the foot-sore Elves around a campfire. Sometimes, perhaps, he brings them a haunch of venison—this Valar, we're sure, makes a mean venison casserole.

continued on the following page ⇒

Here a hearty winter casserole—made in a slow cooker—is elevated to something special by adding a crispy puff pastry topping. It's delicious served with roasted parsnips and baby carrots. For an easier version, skip the pie topping and serve the venison with mashed or boiled, mint-flecked potatoes instead.

Serves 4–5
Prep + cook time 8½–10½ hours

2 tablespoons butter

1 tablespoon olive oil, plus extra
  for greasing

1½ lb. venison, diced

1 onion, chopped

2 tablespoons all-purpose flour

⅔ cup red wine

¾ cup lamb or beef stock

3 medium raw beets, peeled and cut
  into ½-inch dice

1 tablespoon redcurrant jelly

1 tablespoon tomato paste

10 juniper berries, roughly crushed

3 sprigs of thyme

1 bay leaf

7-oz. sheet ready-rolled puff pastry

beaten egg, for glazing

salt and pepper

1. Preheat the slow cooker on low if necessary; see the manufacturer's instructions.

2. Heat the butter and oil in a large skillet, add the venison a few pieces at a time until all the pieces are in the pan, then fry, stirring, until evenly browned. Scoop the venison out of the pan with a slotted spoon and transfer to the slow-cooker pot. Add the onion to the pan and fry for 5 minutes until softened.

3. Stir in the flour, then mix in the wine and stock. Add the beet, redcurrant jelly, and tomato paste, then the juniper, two sprigs of the thyme, and the bay leaf. Season with salt and pepper and bring to a boil. Pour the sauce over the venison, cover with the lid, and cook on low for 8–10 hours, or until tender.

4. Unroll the pastry and trim the edges to make an oval similar in size to the slow-cooker pot. Transfer to an oiled cookie sheet, flute the edges, and add leaves cut from the trimmings. Brush with egg, sprinkle with the remaining thyme leaves stripped from the stem and coarse salt, and bake in the oven at 425°F for about 20 minutes until well risen and golden.

5. Stir the venison and spoon onto plates. Cut the pastry into wedges and place on top of the venison.

Indis's Carrot and Apple Nut Roast

The Elves, as we know, are far from being vegetarian, let alone vegan, but perhaps a few—those Vanyar or Laiquendi perhaps who are especially devoted to the Vala Yavanna, "Giver of Fruits," may have adopted a more 'green' diet, cherishing animal life and using only those fruits, nuts, and vegetables they could gather in the wild.

We have named this dish for Indis, the niece of Ingwë, the King of the Vanyar and High King of all the Elves. She was briefly unhappily married to the Noldor Finwë, the High King of the Noldor. After her husband's death at the hands of Melkor, she returns to her people in Valinor with one of her daughters. The remainder of her children, including Fingolfin (page 53), take part in the Flight of the Noldor.

⌐━ ⋯ ━⌐

Colorful vegetables, sharp apple, crunchy nuts, and fragrant herbs wrapped up in layers of crisp phyllo pastry—this is a vegan delight that will win over even the meat eaters! Serve with green beans and roasted cherry tomatoes.

Serves 4
Prep + cook time 1 hour

3 tablespoons canola oil

1 onion, finely chopped

½ red bell pepper, finely chopped

1 celery stick, finely chopped

1 carrot, peeled and coarsely grated

¾ cup cremini mushrooms, trimmed
  and finely chopped

1 green apple, cored and grated

1 teaspoon yeast extract

1 cup fresh white bread crumbs

⅔ cup mixed nuts, such as pistachios,
  blanched almonds, and cooked
  chestnuts, finely chopped

2 tablespoons pine nuts

2 tablespoons chopped Italian parsley

1 tablespoon chopped rosemary

1 tablespoon whole-wheat flour

8 sheets of phyllo pastry

1. Heat 1 tablespoon of the oil in a skillet, add the onion, red pepper, and celery, and cook over gentle heat for 5 minutes until softened. Add the carrot and mushrooms, and cook for an additional 5 minutes until all the vegetables are tender.

2. Remove the pan from the heat and stir in the grated apple, yeast extract, bread crumbs, nuts, pine nuts, parsley, rosemary, and flour. Season with salt and pepper, and mix together.

3. Brush one sheet of phyllo pastry with some of the remaining oil, then place a second on top. Spoon a fourth of the nut mixture onto one end of the phyllo pastry and roll up, tucking in the ends as you roll to encase the filling. Put seam side down on a cookie sheet. Repeat with the remaining pastry and filling to make four rolls. Brush the tops with the rest of the oil.

4. Bake the parcels in the oven at 375°F for 20 minutes until golden and crisp.

Thranduil's Beef Casserole

The Elves of Greenwood the Great—otherwise known as Mirkwood—seem to have heartier appetites than most of their kindred. In *The Hobbit*, when Bilbo and his companions first come across the Greenwood Elves, they are gathered around a fire, sitting on sawn tree trunks, roasting meat and drinking—rather more like Boy Scouts than we might expect in this remote region of Middle-earth. The Elvenking—who we learn elsewhere is the Sindarin lord Thranduil, father of Legolas—also seems rather less than ethereal, being very partial to red wine (see page 157). Tolkien seems to be at pains to depict his Elves to be very different, earthier beings from the Victorian conception of fairies that he knew from his childhood.

This recipe brings together beef and wine in a hearty recipe that I like to think would have been very popular in the Elvenking's hall.

Slow cookers are wonderful gadgets—a bit of prep, then in go all the ingredients, and you are free to leave the slow cooker bubbling gently away while you get on with your day. All this hearty casserole needs to go alongside is some rice or mashed potato, and perhaps some fine green beans.

Serves 4
Prep + cook time 10½–11½ hours

2 tablespoons olive oil

1¼ lb. stewing beef, trimmed of fat and cubed

¾ cup bacon, diced

10 oz. small shallots

3 garlic cloves, finely chopped

1 tablespoon all-purpose flour

½ cup red wine

1 cup beef stock

1 tablespoon tomato paste

small bunch of mixed herbs or a dried bouquet garni

salt and pepper

chopped parsley, to garnish

1. Preheat the slow cooker on low if necessary; see the manufacturer's instructions.

2. Heat the oil in a large skillet over high heat. Add the beef, a few pieces at a time, until all the beef is in the pan, and cook for 5 minutes, stirring, until browned. Use a slotted spoon to transfer the beef to the slow-cooker pot.

3. Add the bacon and shallots to the skillet and cook over medium heat for 2–3 minutes until the bacon is just beginning to brown. Stir in the garlic and flour, then add the wine, stock, tomato paste, and herbs. Season to taste and bring to a boil, stirring.

4. Pour the sauce over the beef, cover, and cook for 10–11 hours until the beef is tender. Stir and then garnish with chopped parsley.

Salmar's Pork and Mushroom Pasta

Because Tolkien's creation of his legendarium was near lifelong and underwent so many stages of development, his stories of Middle-earth and beyond contain numerous ambiguities, fragments, and mysteries that even his indefatigable editor, his son Christopher Tolkien, was unable to resolve.

One such is the figure of Salmar—a Maia who creates his master Ulmo's sea horns—the Ulumúri—out of conch shells. His name appears just once in *The Silmarillion* and then he seems to have been forgotten. Here's a dish, then, using the conch-shaped conchiglie, to celebrate Salmar and all those intriguing shadows and fragments that so enrich our pleasure as we explore Tolkien's world.

⌐ ··· ⌐

Pour yourself a glass of wine and tuck into a bowl of this richly savory pasta dish topped with plenty of Parmesan. The recipe suggests conchiglie but any hollow shapes, such rigatoni, penne, or orecchiette, which will catch the chunky sauce, would be fine.

Serves 4
Prep + cook time 40 minutes

2 tablespoons olive oil

1 onion, finely chopped

1 garlic clove, finely chopped

14½ oz. ground pork

1 tablespoon tomato paste

¾ cup dry white wine

½ cup hot chicken stock

2 cups mushrooms, trimmed
and chopped

⅓ cup heavy cream

13 oz. conchiglie pasta

⅓ cup Parmesan cheese, grated, plus
extra to serve

salt and pepper

chopped Italian parsley, to garnish

1. Heat 1 tablespoon of the oil in a large skillet, add the onion, and cook for a couple of minutes until beginning to soften. Add the garlic and pork and cook, breaking up the meat with the back of a spoon, for 5–10 minutes, or until the meat is golden.

2. Stir in the tomato paste and cook for an additional minute. Pour over the wine and cook until reduced by half, then add the chicken stock, and simmer for 10 minutes.

3. Heat the remaining oil in a separate skillet. Add the mushrooms and cook for 3 minutes, or until golden and soft. Add to the pork mixture, then stir in the cream.

4. Meanwhile, cook the pasta in a large saucepan of salted boiling water according to the package instructions until al dente. Drain, reserving a little of the cooking water, and return to the pan. Stir through the sauce and Parmesan, adding a little cooking water to loosen if needed. Season well.

5. Spoon into serving bowls and serve sprinkled with the parsley and extra Parmesan.

Karkapolka Sausages

Tolkien was an indefatigable linguist and philologist—by the time he left school he had learned a plethora of languages, not only the (for his class) conventional Latin, Greek, French, Italian, Spanish, and German, but also, among others, Old and Middle English, Gothic, Old Norse, and Medieval Welsh. To these he would add quite a few more through his career as a professor of Anglo-Saxon at Oxford University.

Not content with real-world languages, both living and dead, from early on he also invented his own, most notably Quenya and Sindarin, each of which went through several phases of evolution—like any real language, indeed, but through the wit and imagination of a single mind, gathering rich, fiendishly complex layers of grammar and vocabulary, phonetics and orthography.

So it comes as no surprise to discover that we know two 'Early Quenya' words for 'wild boar'—*úro* and *karkapolka*—the latter derived from the Quenya words for 'tusk' and 'pig' and, in Late Quenya, spelled carcapolca. Take your pick when you serve up this dish to your friends and they ask for the name of the recipe.

When you can't face washing a lot of dishes, this one-pot warming casserole is the recipe to go for. Packed with vegetables and lentils for a delicious and balanced meal, it's a real crowd-pleaser. You could replace the wild boar sausages with venison sausages, if you like.

Serves 4
Prep + cook time 1 hour

8 wild boar sausages, 1 lb. 1 oz.
in total
2 tablespoons olive oil
1 onion, chopped
½ cup red wine
2 cups beef stock
2 tablespoons cranberry sauce
1 tablespoon tomato paste
2 bay leaves
2 cups potatoes, cut into 1-inch
chunks
2 carrots, cut into ¾-inch chunks
1½ cups tomatoes, roughly chopped
4 cups red cabbage, finely shredded
13-oz. can green lentils, rinsed and
drained
salt and pepper

1. Cook the sausages under a medium broiler for 5 minutes, turning until browned but not cooked through.

2. Meanwhile, heat the oil in large flameproof casserole or heavy-bottomed saucepan over medium heat. Add the onion and cook for 4–5 minutes until just softened. Add the red wine, stock, cranberry sauce, tomato paste, and bay leaves, then season to taste and bring to a boil, stirring.

3. Add the potatoes, carrots, tomatoes, red cabbage, and sausages. Cover and simmer for 30 minutes, or until the sausages and potatoes are cooked through. Add the lentils and cook for an additional 5 minutes. Serve in shallow bowls.

Rivendell Roast Lamb

Tolkien's conception of the Elves could change according to his dramatic needs or the readership he had in mind. In *The Hobbit*—a novel written for children with elements of adventure, comedy, and fairy tale—even the Elves are mined for laughs. Just before Bilbo, Gandalf, and the Dwarves reach Elrond's house in Rivendell, they come across a party of Elves singing and cooking out in the open over open fires. Even though the Elves living in the Hidden Valley are largely Noldor and supposedly high-minded, they seem rather frivolous compared to their kindred in *The Lord of the Rings*: their songs are nonsensical and their jibes teasing—even Thorin's venerable beard becomes the object of their fun.

However, for all their merriment, they are hospitable to the new arrivals, even if these are largely made up of Dwarves, inviting them to join their al fresco dinner. The Dwarves rather roughly decline, wanting to reach Elrond's house where perhaps a better meal is on offer. We might have preferred to stay, however, and sup with the boisterous Elves—especially if this roast lamb was on the menu!

Roast lamb gets an Italian twist here with rice, succulent semi-dried tomatoes, peppers, and plenty of garlic combining for a flavor sensation.

Serves 4
Prep + cook time 1¾ hours

2 red bell peppers, deseeded and
   halved
⅔ cup wild rice, cooked
5 garlic cloves, chopped
5 semi-dried tomatoes, chopped
2 tablespoons chopped Italian parsley
1¼ lb. boneless leg of lamb, butterflied
4 artichoke halves
salt and pepper

1. Put the pepper halves in a roasting pan and cook in the oven at 350°F for 20 minutes until the skin has blackened and blistered. Cover with damp paper towels and set aside. When the peppers are cool enough to handle, peel off the skin and chop the flesh. (Leave the oven on.)

2. Mix together one of the chopped peppers, the rice, garlic, tomatoes, and parsley. Season to taste.

3. Put the lamb on a board and make a horizontal incision, almost all the way along, to make a cavity for stuffing. Fold back the top half, spoon in the stuffing, and fold back the top. Secure with skewers.

4. Cook the lamb for 1 hour, basting frequently, and adding the artichokes and other pepper for the last 15 minutes of cooking time. Slice the lamb and serve immediately.

Hunting and Gathering
with the Elves

Hunting and gathering was successfully practiced by us human beings for millions of years before the development of agriculture. It combined the collection of nuts, fruits, roots, vegetables, eggs, and seafood with the scavenging of meat from already-dead animals and also, increasingly, the hunting of live ones. Many early peoples also probably used what is known as forest gardening—the nurturing of existing edible plant species in a woodland and forest setting—to create a kind of natural larder and more dependable food source. Even after the Neolithic or Agricultural Revolution some 11,000 to 12,000 years ago, humans continued to supplement agricultural produce with some hunting and gathering, with hunting increasingly practiced by elites alone.

Tolkien's Elves, who begin their existence in the far east of Middle-earth, seem to have begun their existence as hunter-gatherers, collecting fruits and berries from the wooded shores of Cuiviénen, a gulf on the Inland Sea of Helcar, as well as seafood from the waters. Tolkien portrays this era in the existence of the Elves as a kind of lost age of innocence and plenty—the way, indeed, in which the Eldar themselves seem to have perceived it, as expressed in their saying "And to Cuiviénen there is no returning." There are no doubt comparisons to be drawn between Cuiviénen and the Garden of Eden, both symbolic of an atavistic nostalgia for a lost original home where nature itself spontaneously provided all wants and needs.

The Elves also probably practiced hunting and gathering during the Great Journey into the West. Since they were on the move and ignorant of the landscapes they were passing through, finding enough to eat would have been much more challenging, necessitating the supply of waybread—*coimas* in Quenya—to the Elves by the Vala Oromë. The Elves who reached Aman were no doubt taught agriculture by the Valar, especially by Yavanna and her followers. Among the Elves who remained in Beleriand, we might conjecture that the Sindar of Doriath practiced a kind of forest gardening, as taught to them by the Maia Melian and perhaps by the Ent-wives too, while the Falathrim—the Teleri

of Beleriand's coast—no doubt became expert fishermen. It seems likely that, throughout the long ages, the Sindarin Elves of Middle-earth never gave up hunting and gathering and practiced agriculture only on the smallest of scales, as witnessed in the growing of corn for coimas/lembas bread in small forest clearings. For the Noldor—who went to Valinor but who returned to Middle-earth as exiles—hunting seems to have become an almost aristocratic pursuit, though there is little indication of social hierarchy among Tolkien's Elves, even if there are clearly leading families and dynasties.

Tolkien tells us little or nothing about how the Elves produce their food in *The Lord of the Rings*—but, in the Elvish meal eaten by the Hobbits at Woody End and subsequent ones in Lothlórien, we get the sense that such food—gained whether by hunting and gathering, forest gardening, or small-scale agriculture—always arose out of the Elves' thorough understanding of, and collaboration with, the natural world around them.

Feasting and Sharing

Feasts and feasting are commonplace among almost all the peoples of Middle-earth, the Elves included. Unsurprisingly, as in the real world, feasting and sharing food have been a hallmark of societies for thousands of years. As a renowned Anglo-Saxon scholar, Tolkien knew well how, in Germanic cultures as elsewhere, feasts established or consolidated societal connections and obligations, bringing together host and guest, kin and stranger, even friend and enemy—with the shared meal a symbol of unity and fraternity. In Anglo-Saxon culture the mead-hall where drink and food flowed easily stood at the fulcrum of a flourishing, functioning society.

In Elvish Beleriand, Tolkien constructed a world much like Anglo-Saxon England or Viking Scandinavia, in which a complex network of kings and kingdoms is tied together by kinship and marriage yet threatened by rivalry and enmity. As we see in the Feast of Reuniting (page 120), held by the Noldorin king Fingolfin, feasting is one way in which the Elves smooth over their differences and forge new alliances—even if tensions are never far below the surface.

In this section we've brought together a host of Elvish feasting dishes—from Arwen's Wedding Feast Dish to Egladil Zucchini Fritters—to help you woo your friends and family, and maybe even an enemy or two! Food is the ultimate conciliator—by sharing food we recognize our common humanity or, in the case of the Eldar, our Elven-kinship. Almien!—Cheers!—as Tolkien fans say.

Valinorian Potatoes

The Hobbit Samwise Gamgee may pine for home-grown "tatties" freshly dug from the Gaffer's garden at Number 3, Bagshot Row, but we think that Valinor is the real home of the potato. In the real world, as we all know, the wild potato was first domesticated by Native Americans some 10,000 years ago in the region of what is now Peru. By the time of the Inca—in the fourteenth and fifteenth centuries—potatoes had become the staple food of the region, stored up through the year either by dehydration or fermentation as tocosh. Today there are thousands of potato varieties in Peru alone, in all sorts of colors and sizes—far beyond the Gaffer's dreams, certainly.

This simple potato sharing dish might well have been served at festivals in Valinor, eaten by Valar and Elves alike as they meet in meadows beneath the walls of the capital city, Valmar, something like the Inca Cusco, a fabled city of golden roofs. Sam, after his journey across the Sundering Seas, will be in for a real treat!

―・・―

Hot, crunchy, cheesy potato skins and a creamy, chive-flecked dip—everyone will love this. Serve with pre-dinner drinks and watch it disappear in a flash! If you're pushed for time, then you can use ready-made tzatziki or salsa for dipping instead.

Serves 6
Prep + cook time 15 minutes, plus potato baking

6 large potatoes, baked and left
   to go cold
2 cups grated cheddar cheese
1 tablespoon olive oil

For the sour cream dip
¾ cup sour cream
1 garlic clove, crushed
1 tablespoon chopped chives
salt and pepper

1. To make the dip, combine the ingredients in a bowl and season to taste.

2. Take the cooled potatoes and cut into quarters. Scoop out and discard the potato flesh (or use for another recipe). Transfer the skins to a bowl, pour over the olive oil, and carefully mix with your hands.

3. Place the skins cut-side down on a baking sheet and cook under a hot broiler for 2 minutes. Turn the skins over and carefully sprinkle a little cheese onto each skin. Cook for an additional 2 minutes until the cheese is melted.

4. Serve immediately with the dip.

Egladil Zucchini Fritters

In *The Lord of the Rings*, to bid farewell to the Fellowship, Celeborn and Galadriel hold a feast on the grass at Egladil—the angle of land between the Rivers Anduin and Celebrant. Although it is the only time that the Lord and Lady of Lothlórien eat with their guests during their stay, Tolkien says nothing of the food and drink served, perhaps because Frodo—through whose eyes we largely see the feast—is absorbed by thoughts of the quest to come and eats and drinks very little. We are free to imagine, then, what dishes are set before the Fellowship . . .

These zucchini fritters are quintessentially Elvish—the very freshest and best produce simply prepared to provide the maximum flavor. Eat these and imagine the mallorn trees towering above your head and clusters of golden Elanor flowers at your feet.

⌐—··—⌐

Crispy on the outside and creamy inside, these little zucchini fritters are the perfect snack for sharing. Serve straight from the pan with the sour cream dip on page 104 or with sweet chili sauce for dipping. You can add some finely chopped mint or swap out the Parmesan for feta.

Serves 8
Prep + cook time 30 minutes

8 zucchini, trimmed and grated
8 tablespoons self-rising flour
1 cup Parmesan cheese, grated
4 tablespoons olive oil

1. Place the grated zucchini on a clean dish towel and squeeze out any excess moisture. Place in a bowl with the flour and grated Parmesan and mix together well.

2. Squeeze into walnut-sized balls and then gently flatten each one.

3. Heat the oil in a deep skillet and, working in batches, fry the fritters for 2–3 minutes on each side until golden.

Coimas

Coimas is the original lembas bread—given to the Elves by Oromë for their journey westward across Middle-earth en route to Valinor. This Quenya word means 'life-bread," implying its key role in sustaining and nurturing the Elves during their long trek. The bread was made from the corn (wheat) of Yavanna, so it also seems to have had a sacred quality, too—something akin to the manna provided by God to the Israelites during their forty-year journey through the wilderness on their way to Canaan, the Promised Land.

⌐─··─⌐

An irresistible combination of fluffy, chewy bread, oozy melted cheese, and a runny baked egg, these meal-in-one breads are a little fiddly to prepare but absolutely worth it.

Serves 3
Prep + cook time 40 minutes, plus proofing

For the dough

⅔ cup warm water, plus up to ⅔ cup extra

1 tablespoon active dry yeast

9 cups all-purpose flour, plus extra for dusting

⅔ cup warm milk

⅓ cup olive oil

1 extra-large egg

1 teaspoon granulated sugar

1 teaspoon fine salt

For the filling

1 cup mozzarella cheese, grated

¾ cup feta cheese, crumbled

pinch of cayenne pepper

1 egg, beaten, for brushing

3 eggs, for filling

1. In a small bowl, combine the measured warm water with the yeast. In a large bowl, mix together the remaining dough ingredients and add the yeast mixture. Knead by hand or with a dough hook until it forms a smooth, elastic dough. Add up to ⅔ cup extra warm water if needed. Cover with plastic wrap and leave to rise in a warm place for 2 hours.

2. To make the filling, combine both cheeses and add a pinch of cayenne pepper.

3. Turn out the dough onto a lightly floured surface. Punch down the dough and divide into three pieces. Cover with greased plastic wrap and leave to rest for 15 minutes.

4. Roll each piece of pastry into an oval. Spoon a third of the filling into the center and spread out, leaving a 1-inch border around the edges. Pull the edges of the pastry around the filling and twist the ends to form a boat shape. Place on a cookie sheet lined with baking parchment.

5. Brush the pastry with the beaten egg and bake in the oven at 400°F for 12–15 minutes. Remove the breads from the oven, make a shallow indentation in the filling of each, and crack in an egg. Return to the oven and bake for 3–4 minutes, or until the eggs are set to your liking.

Starlight Tabbouleh

Tolkien's Elves are closely associated with stars and starlight. The Firstborn first awoke under the stars—before the making of the Sun and the Moon—and lived for many years solely by starlight. When the Vala Oromë first comes across the Elves he calls them the Eldar, meaning "of the stars." Even after the Sun and Moon appear in the sky, the Elves retain their love of and affinity with starlight, as we see in the portrayal of the Elf-maid Lúthien, who is first seen by Beren dancing at moonrise in the forest of Doriath, her eyes "as grey as the starlit evening."

In some ways, in portraying the Elves, at least in their origins, as nocturnal beings, he overturns the usual association of night with evil—here the starlit sky is associated with peace, harmony, and closeness to the divine. In this simple dish, jewel-like white pomegranate seeds are used to represent the stars above Middle-earth.

Loaded with lovely flavors, this Middle Eastern salad is made with chopped green herbs and bulgur wheat, and is perfect to share at barbecues as a delicious side to grilled chicken, fish, and meat. If you can't find white pomegranate seeds, red will do just fine.

Serves 4
Prep + cook time 15 minutes, plus cooling

2 cups bulgur wheat
4 tablespoons each chopped cilantro, parsley, and mint
2 tomatoes, diced
3 tablespoons extra-virgin olive oil
3 tablespoons red wine vinegar
¾ cup white pomegranate seeds
salt and pepper

1. Cook the bulgur wheat according to the package instructions. Drain well, put into a serving bowl, and set aside to cool slightly.

2. Stir in the cilantro, mint, parsley, tomatoes, oil, and vinegar, and season with some salt and pepper. Sprinkle with the pomegranate seeds and serve.

A Dish for Aragorn and Arwen's Wedding

Packed full of flavor and layering richly savory and colorful vegetables, this vegetarian moussaka is topped with a creamy yogurt and feta layer, instead of the more traditional béchamel. Serve it with garlic bread and salad or with wilted kale or spinach.

Serves 4
Prep + cook time 1 hour 10 minutes

5 tablespoons olive oil

1 onion, chopped

2 garlic cloves, finely chopped

5 cups zucchini, cut into chunks

3 cups closed cup mushrooms, quartered

1 red bell pepper, cut into chunks

1 orange bell pepper, cut into chunks

2 x 13-oz. cans chopped tomatoes

2 rosemary stems, leaves stripped from stems

½ tablespoon finely chopped thyme leaves

1 teaspoon superfine sugar

2 eggplants, sliced

3 eggs

2 cups Greek-style yogurt

large pinch of grated nutmeg

⅔ cup feta cheese, grated

salt and pepper

1. Heat 1 tablespoon of the oil in a skillet, add the onion, and fry for 5 minutes, stirring, until just beginning to go brown. Add the garlic, zucchini, mushrooms, and peppers and fry for 2–3 minutes.

2. Stir in the tomatoes, rosemary, thyme, sugar, and season with salt and pepper. Bring to a boil, then cover, and simmer for 15 minutes. Tip into a shallow ovenproof dish, leaving enough space to add the eggplant and topping.

3. Meanwhile, heat 2 tablespoons of the oil in a clean skillet and fry half the eggplant slices until softened and golden on both sides. Arrange, overlapping, on top of the tomato mixture. Repeat with the remaining eggplant slices and oil.

4. Stir the eggs, yogurt, nutmeg, and a little pepper together in a bowl, then pour over the eggplant. Sprinkle with the feta and bake in the oven at 350°F for 30–35 minutes until piping hot.

Tolkien is primarily a writer of epic and myth—the world of *The Hobbit*, *The Lord of the Rings*, and even *The Silmarillion* is largely oriented toward male friendship and masculine military virtues such as bravery and loyalty. However, there are also powerful elements of romance—in the love stories of, among others, Beren and Lúthien, Eärendil and Elwing, Faramir and Éowyn, and Aragorn and Arwen—not forgetting, of course, that of Sam Gamgee and the farmer's daughter Rosie Cotton. In some ways, *The Lord of the Rings* ends like a Victorian novel, with a flurry of weddings signaling the restoration of peace and order after a period of strife and uncertainty.

The marriage of the Dúnedain king Aragorn and the Half-elven princess Arwen on Midsummer's Day TA 3019 has an especially symbolic role in this respect: after the end of the War of the Ring, their wedding ushers in a new age, reconciling the lands and peoples of western Middle-earth. In one sense, their union redeems that of their mutual ancestors Beren and Lúthien, which ended tragically and is part of the events that lead to the catastrophic close of the First Age.

This crowd-pleasing dish could well have been served at Arwen's wedding banquet in the halls of Minas Tirith, bringing together, as it does, some of Gondor's finest, Mediterranean-like produce—vibrant vegetables and strong-flavored herbs. See in a bright new age and celebrate the nuptials of the king and queen of the reunited kingdom.

Mereth Aderthad Paella

Here is another celebration dish whose vibrant colors and intense flavors will bring your hurrying guests to the table. We have named it for the Mereth Aderthad, the Feast of Reuniting, held by Fingolfin, the King of the Noldor, soon after the beginning of the First Age. All the Elves of Beleriand, both Noldor and Sindar, attend, and the harmony and friendship that prevail there seems to herald a period of peace and goodwill, free from the threat of the Dark Lord, Morgoth. As we know, things do not turn out quite as planned. Such feasts of apparent unity but hidden rivalries abound in myth and epic, of course—from the *Nibelungenlied* to Arthurian romance—but perhaps this dish will make sure that, at your feast at least, all things go smoothly.

A vegetarian take on the classic Spanish paella, this is a great meal to share with friends. Pile it up on a large platter, place it in the center of the table, add a big green salad, and let everyone dig in.

Serves 4
Prep + cook time 45 minutes

4 tablespoons olive oil

1 onion, chopped

pinch of saffron threads

1 cup arborio rice

4 cups vegetable stock

6 oz. fine asparagus spears, trimmed, and cut into 2-inch lengths

bunch of scallions, cut into strips

1 cup midi plum tomatoes on the vine, halved

1 cup frozen peas

3 tablespoons slivered almonds, toasted

3 tablespoons chopped Italian parsley

salt

1. Heat 1 tablespoon of the oil in a large, heavy-bottomed skillet, add the onion and saffron, and cook over medium heat, stirring frequently, for 5 minutes, until the onion is softened and golden. Add the rice and stir well, then season with some salt. Add the stock and bring to a boil, then cover and simmer, stirring occasionally, for 20 minutes until the stock is almost all absorbed and the rice is tender and cooked through.

2. Meanwhile, heat the remaining oil in a separate skillet, add the asparagus and scallions, and cook over medium heat for 5 minutes until softened and lightly charred in places. Remove from the pan with a slotted spoon. Add the vine tomatoes to the pan and cook for 2–3 minutes on each side until softened.

3. Add the peas to the rice and cook for an additional 2 minutes, then add the asparagus, scallions, and tomatoes, and gently toss through. Sprinkle with the almonds and parsley and serve.

Food for the Great Journey: Outdoor Cooking

Tolkien's Elves have many homes and homelands but they are above all migrants, travelers, and wanderers. When we first encounter a party of Elves in *The Lord of the Rings* they are journeying through the quieter, wooded places of the Shire, camping, cooking, and eating out in the wild.

The story of the Elves begins, indeed, with the Great Journey, when, at the bequest of the Valar, the majority of the Firstborn make their trek from the far east of Middle-earth toward the far west in the days when the Sun and the Moon had not yet risen. It's a journey that is echoed through the aeons of Elvish history—in the Flight of the Noldor across the Helcaraxë (page 53) and the diaspora of the Eldar during the Wars of Beleriand.

Tolkien tells us that the Valar helped sustain the Elves during their journey with coimas bread (page 108) made from the corn of Yavanna—the prototype of the lembas made by the Elves ever after. No doubt, the Elves supplemented this with other hunted and foraged foods, too—so here we have commemorated the Great Journey with a selection of dishes which, while you will likely make them on the barbecue in your own backyard, will evoke something of the adventure of the Elves' starlit march.

Summer means barbecues: warm days, light-filled evenings, friends, laughter, and great food cooked on the fire. These recipes will get your barbecue off to a sizzling start. With a choice of spicy chicken or minted lamb kebabs, lemony mackerel, and a medley of vegetables transformed into colorful skewers, plus herby tabbouleh to serve on the side, there's something to please everyone. Just add ice-cold drinks!

Nandor Barbecued Chicken

In *The Silmarillion* and elsewhere, Tolkien describes how some of the Elves who took part in the Great Journey turned aside from their path—sometimes out of fear of the awe-inspiring natural features they came across, such as the Misty Mountains, sometimes out of wonder at the beauty of Middle-earth. Among the Elves who abandoned the march were some of the Teleri who, led by Lenwë, went southward on reaching the Great River, settling in the woodlands in the Vales of Anduin. They became known as the Nandor—"Those who go back"—some of whom would later settle in Lothlórien.

Perhaps it was at this early stage that the Nandor started to build treehouses—primitive versions of the tree-mansions of Lothlórien. They were adept woodcrafters and skilled with bow and arrow. Here we have imagined a dish perfect for a woodland supper, using meat shot during the day's hunting. Chicken is used in this recipe, but for a more authentic touch you could use pheasant breast.

The fragrant smoke is drifting up slowly to the treetops where it mingles with the stars . . . Perhaps, given the fate of so many of the Elves who reached Beleriand and beyond, the Nandor didn't make such a bad choice after all.

Serves 6
Prep + cook time 20 minutes, plus marinating

1 lb. skinless chicken thigh fillets, cut into thin strips
2 garlic cloves, crushed
2 teaspoons peeled and grated fresh ginger
1 red bird's-eye chili, deseeded and finely chopped
grated rind of 1 lime
2 tablespoons light soy sauce
1 tablespoon sesame oil
1 teaspoon superfine sugar
¼ teaspoon black pepper
6 large lemongrass stalks

1. Place the chicken thighs in a shallow nonmetallic dish. Combine all the remaining ingredients except for the lemongrass stalks and leave to marinate for 1 hour.

2. Peel and discard a few of the outer layers of the lemongrass stalks so that they are a little finer. Cut the thinner end into a point and thread the marinated chicken onto each stalk at this end, zigzagging backward and forward as you go. Cook on a hot barbecue or under a hot broiler for 3–4 minutes on each side, brushing with the marinade halfway through. Serve hot.

Belegaer Barbecued Mackerel

Tolkien tells us how the Teleri arrived too late on the shores of Belegaer to be ferried across the Great Sea and so had to wait for Ulmo's return with the island-raft Tol Eressëa (page 45). Befriended by the Maia Ossë, they fell in love with the sea and so became known as the Sea-elves. Perhaps the sea reminded them of the Inland Sea of Helcar where the Elves had first awakened.

It is not hard to imagine the Teleri sitting round campfires on the beach as they waited under the starlight with the sound of the waves all around them. They were famous singers, too—so their voices would have melded with the rush and roar of the sea. From time to time they would have caught fish and roasted them simply over their fires. No wonder, then, that—when Ulmo finally returned—a large number chose to stay in Middle-earth.

Serves 4
Prep + cook time 20 minutes

4 mackerel, about 13 oz. each
olive oil, for brushing
3 lemons, thinly sliced, plus
   2 tablespoons lemon juice
salt and pepper

1. Slash each mackerel 3–4 times on each side with a sharp knife. Brush with a little oil and season inside and out with salt and pepper. Using cooking string, tie three lemon slices on each side of the fish. Brush the lemon with a little oil and cook the mackerel on a hot barbecue, or under a hot broiler, for 4–5 minutes on each side until lightly charred and cooked through. Set aside to rest for 5 minutes before serving.

Vanyarin Barbecue Lamb

The fair-headed kindred of Elves known as the Vanyar are easily forgotten as we, Tolkien's readers, become embroiled in the tales of the Noldor and the Teleri, and the Wars of Beleriand. Of all the Elves, however, they come closest to completing the Great Journey in its fullest sense: not content with reaching the shores of Aman, they eventually move to the Valinorian capital, Valmar, to live alongside the Valar, in the full light of the Two Trees.

We learn very little of the Vanyar, except for a few of their names, but of all the Elves they live the most settled and peaceful lives. For all their beauty and nobility, they perhaps live the simplest lives, farming the rich soils of Valinor and raising sheep and cattle. When their work was done, they may have eaten dinner out in the open air, roasting meats in their meadows, drinking the meadlike miruvórë, and reciting their exquisite poetry.

Serves 4
Prep + cook time 15 minutes,
  plus chilling

1 lb. boneless leg of lamb, ground
1 small onion, finely chopped
1 garlic clove, crushed
1 tablespoon chopped rosemary
6 anchovies in oil, drained and
  chopped
olive oil, for brushing
salt and pepper

1. Combine the lamb, onion, garlic, rosemary, anchovies, and some salt and pepper in a bowl and use your hands to work them together. Divide into 12 and shape into even-sized, sausage-shaped patties. Chill for 30 minutes.

2. Thread the patties onto metal skewers, brush lightly with oil, and cook on a barbecue or under a hot broiler for 3–4 minutes on each side until cooked through. Serve hot.

Blue Mountains Vegetable Skewers

Ered Luin—or the Blue Mountains—was the second great chain of mountains that the Elves had to negotiate to reach the shores of the Belegaer, the great western ocean. Beyond the mountains lay Beleriand, which at this time lay empty under the starlight. The Blue Mountains were less mighty than the Misty Mountains, but were still a daunting prospect.

We can well imagine how at this point supplies might have been running low, even of the wonderful coimas (page 108). To supplement their diet, the Elves may well have foraged for wild vegetables and herbs in the upland forests and meadows of the mountains, roasting them over their fires after their day's trek. The heady fragrance of the rosemary would have raised their spirits—their long march would soon be over.

Serves 4
Prep + cook time 30 minutes,
plus marinating

3 tablespoons olive oil

1 tablespoon chopped rosemary

2 zucchini, thickly sliced

1 large red bell pepper, deseeded and quartered

16 button mushrooms, trimmed

16 large cherry tomatoes

salt and pepper

ready-made tzatziki, to serve

1. In a large bowl, combine the oil with the rosemary and some salt and pepper. Add the zucchini, pepper, mushrooms, and cherry tomatoes to the oil, toss well, and marinate for 15 minutes.

2. Thread the vegetables onto metal skewers, alternating the vegetables so all the skewers have a good variety.

3. Cook the skewers on a hot barbecue or under a hot broiler for 10–15 minutes, turning halfway through, until all the vegetables are cooked. Serve hot with the tzatziki.

The Great Feast and the Heroic Age of the Elves

Feasts are characteristic of epic literature, found in works from *The Odyssey* of the ancient Greeks and the *Mahābhārata* of ancient India to the *Kalevala* of the Finnish and *Beowulf* of the Anglo-Saxons, so it is unsurprising to find them mentioned frequently in *The Silmarillion*, the collection of tales depicting Middle-earth's heroic First Age. There, as elsewhere, feasts are held for various reasons—celebratory, religious, and reconciliatory. The Valar, we are told, hold a feast to celebrate the end of their labors in forming Arda and another 'high feast" in praise of Eru, the One (the supreme deity). Among the Elves, Fëanor appears at feasts in the Noldor city of Tirion in Aman wearing the Silmarils proudly displayed on his brow, and Fingolfin holds a 'great feast"—known as the Mereth Aderthad (the Feast of Reuniting)—to bring together the Elves of Beleriand in a time of peace and prosperity. Such feasts are often joyous, Tolkien tells us, marked by much music-making and singing and no doubt dancing too, but, sadly, he tells us next to nothing about the food or drink consumed, with the exception of the meadlike cordial miruvórë. Largely, we must imagine these things for ourselves.

Feasts are also a feature of *The Hobbit* and *The Lord of the Rings*, even if it is the intimate meals—the breakfast and the dinner—that we remember best. *The Hobbit* begins with an impromptu 'feast" of the most basic, greedy kind as Thorin and his companions dig into the contents of Bilbo's beloved pantries. The feast proper remains mostly closely associated with the Elves, however—in the halls of Rivendell and the Elvenking. At the beginning of *The Lord of the Rings* the feast is likewise to some extent 'domesticated" as the 'party"—the 'pleasant Feast" celebrating Bilbo's 111st and Frodo's 33rd birthdays and the 'Hundredweight Feast" of the following year held in Bilbo's honor in his absence—and it is only as the narrative itself tips over entirely into the heroic mode, beginning when the Hobbits reach Elvish Rivendell, that 'great feasting" makes its appearance, with a feast to celebrate the victory at the Ford of Bruinen.

Thereafter there is a feast at the departure from Elvish Lothlórien, after which all feasting is at an end until the 'eucatastrophe' of the book's first ending and the midsummer wedding of Arwen and Aragorn. With this celebration—marking the end of the dominion of the Elves and restoration of the dominion of Men—the association of Elves with the 'great feast' comes to an end, though no doubt there are feasts of joy to come in Valinor as the Elves are welcomed to their final homecoming.

Desserts and Sweet Things

Do the Elves have a sweet tooth? From the contents of Bilbo's larder, with its copious supply of pies and cakes, we know that Hobbits do, and from the greed of Thorin and Company when they come to sup with Bilbo so unexpectedly at the beginning of *The Hobbit*, we know that Dwarves do, too. On Men's liking for sweet things we hardly need to pass comment—given their real-world peers. But Elves? Can we really imagine the high-minded Elves, with their taste for poetry and flowers, and combating evil, tucking into anything so frivolous as a lemon meringue pie, a sherry-spiked trifle, or a syrup pudding swimming in custard?

Perhaps not . . . but a fondness for natural sweetness is certainly not beyond the Elvish palate. Quenya has a word for "sweet to the taste"—*lissë*—which seems to refer primarily to the sweetness of honey (the Sindarin equivalent is *leich*). It is used in Galadriel's Lament to describe the mead of the lofty halls of the Valar, and the Elvish drink miruvórë (see pages 148–149) is also described as having a meadlike sweetness. No doubt lissë/leich would also be applied to the sweetness of berries and orchard fruits—which the Elves also seem to savor, if Gildor's impromptu meal enjoyed by Frodo, Pippin, and Sam is anything to go by.

It is honey and fruits, then, that predominate in the following recipes, from Legolas's Bramble Pudding through Hithlum Pie to Yavanna's Fruit Salad. One can be high-minded and indulge oneself from time to time.

Melian's Plum-Topped Cheesecake

We have named this rather sumptuous, alluring cheesecake after the Maia Melian, who in *The Silmarillion* meets and enchants—in both the literal and metaphorical sense—the Telerin Elf Elwë (Thingol) in the nightingale-haunted woods of Nan Elmoth in Beleriand, causing him to forget his people and his journey to Valinor.

In Valinor, Melian has served the two Valar queens Vána and Estë, and in the Gardens of Lórien tended to its many fruit trees. With her dark hair and garments of deep red, she is one of Tolkien's most seductive and sensual characters. As a woodland-dwelling enchantress, she has much in common with the feys of Arthurian legend, most notably Vivienne or Nimuë, who ensorcells the wizard Merlin in the forest of Broceliande.

Plums, then, are a fitting fruit for this enticing, tree-loving enchantress. Taste this fabulous cheesecake and you may well understand why Thingol forgets every thought of his kinsfolk and Valinor. How could they possibly compete?

This creamy baked cheesecake, topped with aromatic poached plums, is sure to be popular with friends and family. Any leftover cheesecake will keep for a few days in the refrigerator and any spare poached plums can be spooned over oatmeal or atop yogurt for breakfast.

Serves 6
Prep + cook time 1 hour, plus cooling and chilling

2 cups ricotta cheese

2 cups cream cheese

2 eggs

1 teaspoon vanilla extract

½ cup superfine sugar

½ small orange

1 teaspoon whole cloves

2 tablespoons dark brown sugar

1 cinnamon stick

½ cup water

2 cups red plums, halved
  and pitted

2 tablespoons redcurrant jelly

1. Grease a 6 x 4-inch loaf pan lightly and line the base and sides with nonstick baking parchment. Blend the ricotta and cream cheese with the eggs, vanilla extract, and superfine sugar until smooth. Turn the mixture into the loaf pan and place in a small roasting pan. Pour hot water into the pan to a depth of 1 inch and bake in the oven at 325°F for about 40 minutes or until lightly set. Lift the loaf pan out of the water and allow the cheesecake to cool in the pan.

2. Meanwhile, stud the orange with the cloves, and place in a heavy-bottomed pan with the brown sugar, cinnamon, and measured water. Bring the water to a boil, reduce the heat, and add the plums. Cover and cook gently for 5 minutes, or until just tender.

3. Lift out the plums and add the redcurrant jelly to the pan. Boil the liquid for about 2 minutes until reduced and syrupy. Remove the orange and cinnamon stick, and pour the syrup over the plums. Let the syrup cool, then chill until ready to serve.

4. Remove the cheesecake from the pan, peel off the paper, and cut into slices. Serve topped with the poached plums.

Dorthonion Heather Honey Sponge

Tolkien mentions honey regularly in his works. Beekeeping appears to be practiced by most of the peoples of Middle-earth, with honey used to sweeten cakes and other foodstuffs and, of course, to make mead. The best-known beekeeper, of course, is the Skin-changer Beorn in *The Hobbit,* who is a dab hand at making honey cakes.

We may conjecture, however, that beekeeping was originally an Elvish activity, which was perhaps taught to them by the Valar in Valinor. In *The Lord of the Rings,* Galadriel sings a lament for the Elves in exile, mourning the memory of the 'sweet mead in lofty halls beyond the West" and the emptiness of her cup in Middle-earth. There is a recording of Tolkien giving a fine rendition of Galadriel's Lament—in the original Quenya, of course.

For this pudding we have specified heather honey, perhaps like that made in Dorthonion, in the north of Beleriand, whose characteristic landscapes were forest and heather-covered heathlands. For some time this was the kingdom of the Noldorin Elves Angrod and Aegnor, until it was overrun by Morgoth after the Dagor Bragollach—the Battle of the Sudden Flame.

A great one for lunch boxes, this cake is beautifully sweet because of the honey. You can ring the changes by adding a teaspoon of mixed spice or ground cinnamon to the mix, and it also works really well with pears instead of apples.

Makes a 2-lb. loaf cake
Prep + cook time 1¼ hours

1 cup all-purpose flour

½ cup whole-wheat flour

1 teaspoon baking powder

3 tablespoons superfine sugar

½ cup heather honey, plus extra to serve

½ cup butter, softened

3 eggs, lightly beaten

1 teaspoon vanilla extract

3 tablespoons apple juice

1 large dessert apple, peeled, cored, and chopped

1. Line an 8 x 4-inch loaf pan with nonstick baking parchment. Sift the flours and baking powder into a large bowl. Mix in the sugar, honey, butter, eggs, vanilla extract, and apple juice. Stir through the apple.

2. Spoon the mixture into the prepared pan and bake in the oven at 350°F for 1 hour. To see if it is cooked, insert a skewer in the center of the loaf—if it comes out clean it is done, but if cake mix is attached to the skewer it will need an additonal 10 minutes.

3. Remove the cake from the oven and turn out onto a wire rack. Peel off the baking parchment and leave to cool. Serve cut into slices with a drizzle of honey.

Galadriel's Cookies

Galdariel and cookies . . . unimaginable! But think again: Galadriel is, as Frodo witnesses, not only the majestic queen, Noldorin exile, possessor of the Elven ring Vilya (page 83), and survivor of thousands of years of Elven history, but also wife, mother, and friend, the thoughtful, tender Elf-lady who bestows gifts of both power and simplicity on the Fellowship at their parting—from the Elfstone for Aragorn to a single silver nut of a mallorn tree for Sam. How touching is that gray wooden box marked with a ''G'' that she hands to the awestruck Hobbit?

Here's a simple almond cookie, then, made by Galadriel when she feels like being just a normal Elf-maid, to share with her attendants on a lazy day under the mallorn trees.

When friends come over for coffee, serve up a plate of these crumbly, orange-scented cookies, fresh from the oven. If you swap the all-purpose flour for rice flour and use gluten-free baking powder, then any gluten-intolerant people can safely enjoy them too.

Makes 20
Prep + cook time 20 minutes, plus chilling

½ cup cornmeal

¼ cup all-purpose flour, plus extra
   for dusting

¼ cup ground almonds

½ teaspoon baking powder

½ cup confectioners' sugar

¼ cup butter, cubed

1 egg yolk, beaten

grated rind of 1 orange

⅓ cup slivered almonds

1. Line two cookie sheets with nonstick baking parchment.

2. Place the cornmeal, flour, ground almonds, baking powder, confectioners' sugar, and butter in a food processor and blitz until the mixture resembles fine bread crumbs. Alternatively, mix together the cornmeal, flour, ground almonds, baking powder, and confectioners' sugar in a large bowl, then add the butter and rub in with your fingertips until the mixture resembles fine bread crumbs.

3. Add the beaten egg yolk and orange rind, and combine to form a firm dough. Wrap in plastic wrap and chill in the refrigerator for 30 minutes.

4. Turn the dough out onto a lightly dusted work surface, roll out thinly, and use a 1½-inch cutter to cut out 20 cookies, rerolling the trimmings as necessary. Transfer to the prepared cookie sheets and sprinkle with the slivered almonds.

5. Bake in the oven at 350°F for about 8 minutes until golden. Remove from the oven, leave for a few minutes to harden on the cookie sheets, then transfer to a wire rack to cool completely.

Teiglin Hazelnut and Pear Cake

Hazels appear quite frequently in Tolkien's writings, often come across by his wanderers, questers, and exiles as they scramble through Middle-earth's wild, rugged landscapes. Hazels are known for their soft, downy leaves, pale-golden catkins, and their winter nuts, sometimes known as cobnuts or filberts, according to the species. No doubt such nuts would have been gathered and eaten by every people of Middle-earth, especially when other foodstuffs were scarce. In the real world, protein-rich hazelnuts were often stored or ground up into a meal to add to flour.

There are brakes of hazel growing close to the River Teiglin in Beleriand. It is close to a hazel tree that Tolkien's tragic hero Turin kills Forweg, the captain of a group of outlaws, and then assumes the leadership himself.

Roulades look tricky but are surprisingly easy and very satisfying to make—the trick is to use the baking parchment to help you roll it. This dinner-party dazzler combines a nutty, light-as-air sponge with juicy apricots and rich mascarpone.

Serves 6–8
Prep + cook time 50 minutes, plus cooling

1 cup roasted hazelnuts

5 eggs, separated

¾ cup superfine sugar, plus extra for sprinkling

1 just-ripe pear, peeled and coarsely grated

¾ cup mascarpone cheese

2 tablespoons confectioners' sugar

2 cups fresh apricots, roughly chopped

1. Roughly chop 2 tablespoons of the hazelnuts and reserve, then finely chop the remainder.

2. Whisk the egg yolks and sugar until they are thick and pale and the whisk leaves a trail. Fold in the finely chopped hazelnuts and the pear. Whisk the whites into stiff, moist-looking peaks. Fold a large spoonful into the nut mix to loosen it, then gently fold in the remaining egg whites.

3. Spoon the mixture into the prepared pan. Bake in the oven at 350°F for 15 minutes until golden brown and the top feels spongy. Cover and leave to cool for at least 1 hour.

4. Beat the mascarpone and confectioners' sugar together until soft. On a work surface, cover a damp dish towel with baking parchment and sprinkle with sugar. Turn the roulade onto the paper and remove the pan and lining paper.

5. Spread the roulade with the mascarpone mixture, then with the apricots. Roll up the roulade, starting from the short end nearest you, using the paper and dish towel to help. Transfer the roulade to a serving plate, join side down, sprinkle with the reserved hazelnuts, and cut into thick slices.

Goldberry's Honeycomb Stack

Tolkien fans debate long and hard over the mysterious nature and origin of Tom Bombadil and his wife, Goldberry—kindly, hospitable beings whom Frodo and his companions encounter soon after their departure from the Shire. All we are told is that he is known to the Elves as the "oldest and fatherless" and that she is "daughter of the river"—leaving us to conjecture whether both are nature spirits, perhaps Maiar in the service of Yavanna (see page 7) and Ulmo (see page 50), respectively. Others have suggested that Goldberry is "only" the daughter of a Maia, and we might even hazard that her father was an Elf—just as Lúthien is the daughter of the Maia Melian and the Sindarin Elf Thingol. Indeed, Goldberry is explicitly compared to "a young elf-queen," wreathed in flowers just like Lúthien.

Whatever her origin, Goldberry is closely associated with the bounty of nature. In inviting the Hobbits to stay in the couple's home, Tom conjures up a vision of their household, where Goldberry's table is already laden with, among other delectables, honeycomb and cream, and where roses peep over the windowsills.

These delicious double-decker pancakes are a breeze to make: simply assemble and griddle. Or, for an al fresco treat, you can cook them on the barbecue. Serve topped with blueberries, strawberries, or raspberries.

Serves 2
Prep + cook time 10 minutes

¼ cup heavy cream, plus extra to serve

1½ oz. honeycomb or old-fashioned cinder toffee, crumbled

1 teaspoon finely grated lemon rind

½ cup candied lemon peel, finely chopped (optional)

⅔ cup lemon curd

6 frozen pancakes

1. Put the cream, honeycomb or cinder toffee, lemon rind, candied peel (if using), and lemon curd in a bowl and mix well. Place a dollop of the lemon cream on a pancake, top with a second pancake and another dollop of lemon cream on top, then finish with a third pancake. Repeat the process so that you have two triple-decker lemon pancakes.

2. Cook the pancake stacks on a grill pan over medium-high heat for 1–2 minutes, then carefully flip over and cook for an additional 1–2 minutes until the outside pancakes are toasted, and the lemon cream is beginning to ooze from the sides. Serve immediately.

Vana's Apple Pie

Many of Tolkien's Powers of Arda—his 'gods' and 'goddesses'—can be related to figures in real-world mythologies. This is certainly the case with the beautiful Vána, the younger sister of Yavanna (see page 29), at whose passing flowers spring to life and birds begin to sing. She is clearly related to figures such as the Greek goddesses Persephone—goddess of spring growth—and Hebe—goddess of youth.

Perhaps the closest analogy—one that the Anglo-Saxon specialist Tolkien might have preferred—is with the Norse goddess Iðunn, whose very name may mean 'Ever-young,' a epithet likewise of Vána. Iðunn is best known as the keeper of the apples of youth, which keep the gods young, and Vána, too, dwells in gardens of golden flowers and trees, including, no doubt, fruit trees. This golden dessert is for her, then: imagine the immortal Elves dining al fresco in their own orchards and tucking into this divine confection.

⌐──··──⌐

Sweet, spiced apples combine with flaky puff pastry in this version of the traditional family favorite. Serve it warm with spoonfuls of crème fraîche or extra-thick cream, or a scoop of the Simbelmynë Ice Cream on page 143.

Serves 6
Prep + cook time 45 minutes

2 lb. or about 5 cooking apples, quartered, cored, peeled, and thickly sliced

½ cup superfine sugar, plus extra for sprinkling

grated rind of 1 small orange

½ teaspoon ground mixed spice or ground cinnamon

3 whole cloves

13 oz. chilled ready-made puff pastry

a little flour, for dusting

1 egg, beaten

1. Fill an 8-inch pie pan with the apples. Mix the sugar with the orange rind, mixed spice, and cloves, then sprinkle over the apples.

2. Roll the pastry out on a lightly floured surface until a little larger than the top of the pan. Cut two long strips from the edges, about ½ inch wide. Brush the rim of the pie pan with a little beaten egg, press the strips on top, then brush these with egg. Lift the remaining pastry over the pan and press the edges together well.

3. Trim off the excess pastry, make small, horizontal cuts around the pastry rim with a small knife (this helps encourage the layers in the pastry to separate and rise), then press the edges of the pie together neatly. Reroll the trimmings and cut out small heart shapes or circles with a small cookie cutter. Brush the top of the pie with beaten egg, add pastry shapes, then brush these with egg. Sprinkle with a little extra sugar.

4. Bake in the oven at 400°F for 20–25 minutes until the pastry is well risen and golden.

Hithlum Pie

Here is another Elvish tart, this one using a mixture of honey and pine nuts. Pines are mentioned in Tolkien's works more than any other tree and are characteristic of many highland landscapes across Middle-earth. In the First Age, the cold, misty region of Hithlum, to the northwest of Beleriand, was almost completely surrounded by pine-clad mountains, and they also grew in the vicinity of Rivendell, in the lee of the Misty Mountains, their sweet, resinous smell making Bilbo drowsy as he and the Dwarves draw close to Elrond's home.

The Elves no doubt put every one of Yavanna's gifts to good use, the edible seeds of pine trees—rich in protein and carbohydrates—included. Here they are teamed with a flowery honey to make a filling, tasty pie that would have helped keep out the chill of even the coldest day in Hithlum.

⌐──··──⌐

This unusual pie is a delicately balanced combination of sweet honey and crunchy pine nuts. Serve with ice cream, cream, or a blob of crème fraîche and drizzle with a little extra honey for a nice flourish.

Serves 8–10
Prep + cook time 1 hour
** 20 minutes**

13 oz. chilled ready-made or
   homemade pie pastry
½ cup unsalted butter
½ cup superfine sugar
3 eggs
⅔ cup flower honey, warmed
grated rind and juice of 1 lemon
1½ cups pine nuts

1. Roll out the pastry thinly on a lightly floured surface and line a 9-inch loose-bottomed tart pan. Prick the base, line with nonstick baking parchment, add pie weights or baking beans, and bake blind in the oven at 375°F for 15 minutes. Remove the paper and pie weights, and bake for an additional 5 minutes. Reduce the oven temperature to 350°F.

2. Cream together the butter and superfine sugar. Beat in the eggs, one at a time, then mix in the warmed honey, the lemon rind and juice, and the pine nuts. Pour into the pie case and bake for about 40 minutes until browned and set.

3. Let the pie cool for 10 minutes before serving.

Lemon Meringue and Sea Buckthorn Pies

One of the most glorious sights on Europe's temperate sandy coasts are the banks of sea buckthorn (*Hippophae rhamnoides*), with its clouds of deep orange berries set amid dark green spiny leaves. As a scholar of Old English, Tolkien might have especially appreciated this coastal shrub, which the Anglo-Saxons believed, like hawthorn, to ward off harm and was used on magic charms. The Old English rune *ðorn* (thorn)—was thought to have defensive powers.

We might imagine sea buckthorn growing in the sandy dunes on Middle-earth's northwestern coasts, including in First Age Beleriand, in the region known as Falas (Sindarin for "coast"). The Falathrim—the "Coast-elves"—were doubtless expert foragers and made good use of this tart berry which tastes something like a mixture of orange and mango.

The sublime blend of creamy lemon filling topped with billowy sweet meringue makes this classic pie such a winner. And it is even better served with wonderfully colorful sea buckthorn sauce. Picked fresh, sea buckthorn berries taste very tart, but cook them with a little sugar or maple syrup to sweeten and a taste sensation is revealed.

continued on the following page ⇾

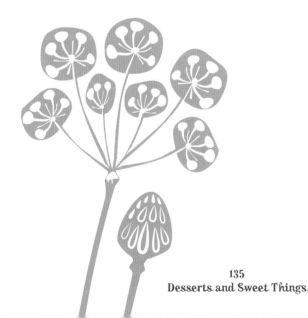

Makes 6
Prep + cook time 1 hour,
plus chilling

12 oz. chilled ready-made or
   homemade pie pastry
13-oz. can full-fat condensed milk
3 egg yolks
grated rind of 2 lemons
4 tablespoons lemon juice
4 egg whites
½ cup superfine sugar

For the sauce
2 cups sea buckthorn berries
2 teaspoons maple syrup
½ cup granulated sugar

1. Grease six individual 4-inch loose-bottomed tart pans. Cut the pastry into six, then roll one portion out on a lightly floured surface and use it to line one of the pans. Press the pastry into the base and sides of the pan, then trim off the excess with scissors so that it stands a little above the top of the pan. Patch any cracks or breaks with pastry trimmings. Repeat to make six pies. Prick the bases with a fork, then chill for 15 minutes. Line each pastry case with nonstick baking parchment, add pie weights or baking beans, and bake in the oven at 375°F for 10 minutes. Remove the paper and pie weights, and bake for an additional 5 minutes.

2. Remove from the oven and reduce the oven temperature to 350°F. Mix the condensed milk, egg yolks, lemon rind, and juice together in a bowl until the mixture thickens, then spoon the filling into the pastry cases. In a second bowl, whisk the egg whites until stiff, then gradually whisk in the sugar, a little at a time, until very thick and glossy.

3. Spoon the meringue over the lemon filling and swirl with the back of a spoon into peaks. Bake for 10–15 minutes until the meringue peaks are golden and just set. Leave to stand for 5 minutes, then remove from the pans and transfer to a serving plate.

4. Meanwhile, make the sauce. Put the berries and maple syrup in a saucepan over medium heat. Add a splash of water and bring to a boil. Turn down the heat, cover, and gently simmer for 10 minutes.

5. Remove from the heat and strain through a sieve into a bowl or jug, using a spoon to push through as much of the juice and pulp as possible.

6. Return the juice to the pan, add the sugar, and cook over low heat, stirring, until the sugar has dissolved. Pour into a jug, allow to cool, and serve with the pies.

Elbereth's Star-Berry Cream

Here is a sweet dish that might be made for feast days in Valinor. Just as in the real world blueberries grow in Canada and the northeastern United States, we may speculate that this low-lying shrub also grew in the north of Valinor, perhaps in the hills about Formenos, the "Northern Fortress" of Fëanor and his sons. The Native Americans have gathered the sky-colored fruit of wild blueberries for thousands of years, calling them "star-berries" for their star-shaped blossoms. They also used blueberry root to make tea.

We have named the cream for Varda, Queen of the Valar, who created the stars and who for this reason was especially venerated by the Elves, who first came into being under starlight. One of her titles is Elbereth, which in Sindarin means "Queen of the Stars." Best eaten outside on a bright, cloudless night.

⌐—••—⌐

These little desserts are lovely accompanied by mini meringues or lemon shortbread. For a banana version, replace the blueberries with two sliced bananas and decorate the finished desserts with a sprinkling of grated dark chocolate.

Serves 6
Prep + cook time 15 minutes, plus cooling

⅔ cup granulated sugar

3 tablespoons cold water

2 tablespoons boiling water

1 cup fresh (not frozen) blueberries

2 cups fromage frais

2 cups ready-made custard

1. Put the sugar and measured cold water into a skillet and heat gently, stirring occasionally until the sugar has completely dissolved. Bring to a boil and cook for 3–4 minutes, without stirring, until the syrup is just changing color and is golden around the edges.

2. Add the measured boiling water, standing well back as the syrup will spit, then tilt the pan to mix. Add the blueberries and cook for 1 minute. Take the pan off the heat and set it aside to cool slightly.

3. Mix the fromage frais and custard together, spoon into small dishes, then spoon the blueberry mixture over the top. Serve immediately.

Legolas's Bramble Pudding

Of all Tolkien's Elves, Legolas is the one we get to know best and the most fully rounded. For the most part, the Elven characters of *The Silmarillion*—with some exceptions such as Thingol, Fëanor, and Lúthien perhaps—remain somewhat remote and "mythological." Even in *The Lord of the Rings* the characters of Elrond, Galadriel, and Arwen are Tolkien stock types (we might even say archetypes)—the wise old man, the powerful queen, and the ever-patient, ever-faithful princess, respectively. Legolas, of course, is also something of an Elvish stereotype—keen-eyed, a superlative archer, somewhat haughty, in tune with nature . . . but he is also a fully fleshed-out character. He even has something of a narrative arc—gaining a wider empathy for the world and its peoples as he leaves behind his native prejudices, as we see in his evolving relationship with the Dwarf Gimli.

Every well-rounded character has a backstory, too, of which the novelist can provide as much as they like and the reader can fill in as much as they choose. So we might like to think of Legolas, as Thranduil's only son, as having a rather closeted childhood, a Sindarin prince kept apart from the Elvenking's lower-born Green-elf subjects. Nonetheless he also has a rebellious streak and, come fall, sneaks out from his father's halls to go berrying in the forest, returning with a full stomach and telltale purple smears around his mouth.

continued on the following page ⇛

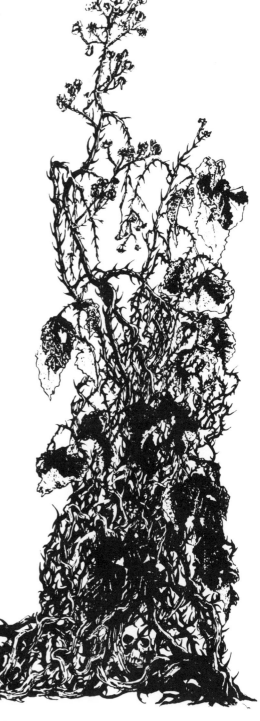

This spin on a conventional trifle is quite versatile: you can enjoy it hot in winter and it's also lovely cold in summer. For a boozy version, stir a splash of brandy or whiskey into the poached fruit mixture.

Serves 4
Prep + cook time 45 minutes, plus cooling

5 oz. fresh or frozen blackberries
2 dessert apples, cored, peeled, and sliced
1 tablespoon water
¼ cup superfine sugar
4 trifle sponges
3 tablespoons dry or sweet sherry
2 cups ready-made custard

For the meringue
3 egg whites
⅓ cup superfine sugar

1. Put the blackberries, apples, measured water, and sugar in a saucepan, then cover and simmer for 5 minutes, or until the fruit has softened. Leave the mixture to cool slightly.

2. Break the trifle sponges into chunks and arrange in an even layer in the base of a 6-inch round pie or soufflé dish, and drizzle with the sherry. Spoon the poached fruit and syrup over the top, then cover with the custard.

3. Whisk the egg whites in a large, dry bowl until stiffly peaking, then gradually whisk in the sugar, a teaspoonful at a time, until the meringue is stiff and glossy. Spoon over the custard and swirl the top with the back of a spoon.

4. Bake in the oven at 350°F for 15–20 minutes until heated through and the meringue is golden. Serve immediately.

Ossë's Dessert

Some of the Valar and Maia are closer, and more sympathetic, to the Elves than others. One such is the Maia Ossë, a servant of Ulmo, Lord of Waters, a spirit who delights in islands and seashores but who has a wild, unpredictable temperament. He has something in common with the minor Greek sea gods such as Triton, Nereus, and Proteus.

During the Great Journey of the Elves west, Ossë befriends some of the Teleri Elves on the shores of the ocean and persuades some, including Círdan (page 21), to remain there, rather than traveling onward to Valinor. He teaches them all the ways of the sea—shipbuilding, navigation, and sea music, and perhaps sea cuisine as well.

We imagine that, originally, this delicious dessert—one of Ossë's specialities—would have been set using caragean—made from the dried seaweed gathered from the wild shores of the Falas—but nowadays agar-agar will do just as well!

⌐——···——⌐

Go retro with this dessert, everyone's childhood favorite. This recipe uses agar-agar, made from seaweed, rather than gelatin, making it suitable for vegans and vegetarians. Using agar-agar gives a much firmer texture than using gelatin, but the result is just as delicious. Serve with raspberries or strawberries and nondairy ice cream.

Serves 4
**Prep + cook time 15 minutes,
  plus standing and setting**

3 cups cranberry juice
4 tablespoons agar-agar flakes
½ cup superfine sugar

1. Pour the cranberry juice into a saucepan and sprinkle in the agar-agar flakes and sugar. Stir, then leave to stand for 10 minutes to allow the agar-agar to soften.

2. Heat over low heat, stirring, until the sugar has dissolved. Bring up to a boil and boil for 1–2 minutes or until the agar-agar has completely melted.

3. Take off the heat and pour into a dessert mold. Leave to cool completely, then chill in the fridge for 4 hours until set. Unmold the dessert onto a serving plate and serve.

Simbelmynë Ice Cream

As we know, Tolkien mostly drew on real-world flora and fauna for the plants and animals of Middle-earth but occasionally invented new, imagined species (page 144). One of these is simbelmynë—called by the Elves uilos or alfirin—a low-growing plant with small white flowers. In *The Silmarillion*, Tolkien records them as growing in a ravine between the Fourth and Fifth Gates on the path to the hidden Elvish city of Gondolin (see page 31). In later ages, the flower often grew on the graves of warrior Men: the word *simbelmynë* means "ever-mind," suggestive of its role as a flower of remembrance, a kind of "forget-me-not."

Tolkien compared the flower to the anemone, but perhaps it also has a resemblance to sweet woodruff, whose white, starlike flowers soldiers once placed inside their helmets for luck on the battlefield—a martial association shared with simbelmynë. Here we use the sweet, fragrant leaves of woodruff to make a delicious, strikingly flavored ice cream.

———···———

Mild and sweet, woodruff—a little-known herb but one well worth growing in your herb garden—adds a delicate grassy note to this ice cream. For a tropical version, replace the woodruff with two star anise.

Serves 6
**Prep + cook time 30 minutes,
  plus infusing and freezing**

1 cup whole milk
14-oz. can full-fat coconut milk
1 cup sweet woodruff leaves
5 egg yolks
⅓ cup superfine sugar

1. Place the milk, coconut milk, and woodruff in a saucepan over low heat and bring just to a boil. Take off the heat and leave to infuse for at least 2 hours. Strain and discard the woodruff leaves.

2. In a bowl, beat the egg yolks with the superfine sugar until pale and creamy. Stir in the milk mixture, then pour into a saucepan. Heat gently, stirring, until the mixture coats the back of a spoon. Take off the heat and allow to cool.

3. Pour into an ice-cream maker and process according to the manufacturer's instructions or pour into a freezer-proof container. Place in the freezer until the edges start to freeze, then remove from the freezer and beat the ice cream vigorously with a fork or electric hand mixer. Return to the freezer and repeat this step at least twice (breaking up the mixture will make your ice cream smooth and creamy), then leave to freeze until ready to serve.

A Botanical Treasure Trove

Tolkien loved nature. As a child he learned botany from his mother and liked nothing better than to ramble through the countryside about his Midlands home, getting to know its plants and flowers. He transposed this love into his writing: when reading *The Lord of the Rings*, as we follow the progress of his characters through the vast and varied landscapes of Middle-earth, we too become immersed in its natural world. We feel the rich earth underfoot in the Shire, we become entangled in the brambles and nettles of the Old Forest, and we gaze across to the haze of the Misty Mountains on the far horizon. We experience every kind of weather—from the unsparing rains that seep through the seams of the travelers' clothes, to the knuckle-blistering blizzards on Mount Caradhras, to the scorching sunshine of southern lands like Gondor.

The reader's imaginative immersion in nature is made possible by Tolkien's meticulous and deeply empathetic descriptions of the living landscapes of his continent and the trees, plants, and herbs that flourish there. Nature, in *The Lord of the Rings* especially, is as much a character as the Hobbits, Men, and Elves who live and depend on it. There is plenty of luminous detail—from the smooth silver-gray bark of the mallorn trees of Lothlórien; to the long, pungent leaves of athelas, or Kingsfoil, used to treat Frodo's Morgul knife wound; to the brakes of old brown fern that Frodo and Sam bed down in the shadows of the mountains of Mordor. Nature feels inhabited—literally so in the case of the Ents, Tolkien's walking trees.

In *The Two Towers*, the Ent Treebeard tells the Hobbits Merry and Pippin about the disappearance of the Entwives, a sad tale told in the songs of Elves and Men. The Ents—a name Tolkien borrowed from the Anglo-Saxon word for "giants"—concerned themselves with shepherding the wild trees of Middle-earth's forests and woods, and were taught to speak with them by the Elves. The Entwives, however, were increasingly drawn to the "lesser" trees—such as the wild cherry and wild apple—domesticating them in their orchards and gardens. The Entwives—who to some extent resemble the helpful dryads (wood nymphs) of Greek mythology—taught the horticultural arts to Men and also, we assume, to the Elves.

Mostly based on the real-world species of northern Europe, the botany of Middle-earth is enriched with species more or less invented, sometimes supernatural—many, like the mallorn and athelas, introduced from Aman or Númenor. Tolkien was also careful to vary his flora from region to region, land to land, so that, for example, each of his forests or woodlands are distinctive from the others. Lothlórien and Fangorn are only a few dozen miles from each other but are entirely different as biomes: the former spacious and bright and full of flowers—the white-flowered niphredil and the golden star-shaped elanor—and the latter dim, musty, cramped—like the Old Took's study, Pippin comments.

How this botanical richness and variety shaped the Elves' culinary heritage we can only guess. To some extent, there would have been staples grown regardless of place or time—the corn grown to make the Elvish waybread; orchard fruits like apples and plums; kitchen gardens of vegetables of much the same kind we find in the Shire—carrots, cabbages, potatoes, and so forth—but these would have been supplemented by more local species and varieties, foraged and gathered, herbs, roots, nuts, mushrooms, and berries.

Drinks

Elves drink for all the reasons humans do—to quench their thirst, for refreshment, to celebrate and make merry, and perhaps even on occasion to forget their worries and woes. There are even hints that in certain circumstances a drink can have a spiritual significance, just as the Elvish waybread lembas does.

Of nonalcoholic drinks miruvórë is the most quintessentially Elvish—a cordial or tonic that made its appearance very early on in the evolution of Tolkien's legendarium. Golden-colored and invigorating, it might be described as magical, though the Elves themselves would be dismissive of that word. For them, everything in nature derives ultimately from Eru Ilúvatar, the All-Father.

Among alcoholic drinks, wine is clearly the drink of choice for the Elves, although every people in Middle-earth—Hobbits, Men, Dwarves, and no doubt Orcs—seem to enjoy a glass or two. The Elves appear to have developed viticulture in the First Age (they may well have learned it from the Valar), and by the Third Age wine is produced and enjoyed in every corner of the continent, from the Shire to Gondor to Rhovanion. Few seem to be such a wine connoisseur, though, as the Elvenking of Greenwood, whose cellars are lined with barrels of the best vintages and who even has a butler-cum-sommelier to take care of them!

Here you will find choice drinks for every occasion—from two versions of miruvórë through a homemade sloe gin to a heady wine punch of which even the Elvenking would have approved.

Gildor's Elderflower Cordial

Soon after the three Hobbit companions—Frodo, Pippin, and Sam—leave the High Elves at Woody End (page 41), they discover that their hosts have thoughtfully filled their water bottles with a delicious drink. Tolkien does not identify the drink—presumably because the Hobbits cannot know what it is—but it does have strong similarities to the revitalizing drink miruvóre (page 147) that turns up quite often in the legendarium.

Tolkien describes the cordial's appearance ("pale golden"), scent (like "honey made of many flowers"), and effects ("wonderfully refreshing") in some detail; it even seems to lift the Hobbits' mood, causing them to laugh and flick their fingers at the rain, though without inebriating them. Perhaps we wouldn't expect anything less of an Elvish drink—the perfect stimulant without side effects or a hangover.

We might conjecture that miruvóre—named for the nectar drink of the Valar, miruvóre—is the exiled Elves' attempt to re-create the elixirs they drank in Valinor, and that they make it in different versions, with whatever ingredients are close to hand. Our version of Gildor's cordial here, then, is made from elderflowers, which would have grown abundantly in the woodlands of the Shire.

—··—

The creamy white flowers of the elder tree make a great cordial. Gather them on a dry day and, before you add them to the cordial, fill a large bowl with cold water and gently swish the elderflower heads in it to get rid of any dirt or insects. You can buy citric acid at some grocery stores and online.

Makes about 1¾ pints
Prep time 10 minutes, plus standing

20 elderflower heads
3 lemons, sliced
5 teaspoons citric acid
4 cups granulated or superfine sugar
1 cup boiling water

1. Put the elderflower heads, sliced lemons, and citric acid in a large heatproof bowl. Dissolve the sugar in the measured boiling water, stirring frequently until dissolved.

2. Add to the bowl of elderflowers. Cover and leave to stand overnight. Strain through a cheesecloth-lined sieve and pour into sterilized bottles. Store in a cool place and use within six months.

Cordial of Imladris

Here is another version of miruvórë, this one inspired by the Cordial of Imladris entrusted by Elrond to Gandalf when the Fellowship of the Ring leaves Rivendell (Imladris in Sindarin). Elrond's cordial is clearly more precious and more potent than Gildor's, since he bestows only a single bottle, whereas, back in the Shire, Gildor liberally filled all three Hobbits' bottles. The Hobbits quaffed back the drink rather cavalierly, it seems, while Gandalf produces Elrond's cordial only in extremis, when the Fellowship is struggling through blizzards on Mount Caradhras. Indeed, he tells his companions that the drink is "very precious" and allows them only a mouthful each—just enough to renew their strength and resolve.

⌐ ·· ⌐

For a refreshing drink, dilute the cordial with water in a ratio of one part cordial to three parts water, adding a few of the sliced lemons for decoration, plus ice cubes and sprigs of fresh mint or lemon balm. And, if serving to adults, you might like to add a splash of vodka or gin.

Makes about 20 glasses
Prep + cook time 20 minutes,
plus cooling

3 unwaxed lemons, washed and very
  thinly sliced

2 tablespoons honey

1 cup fresh ginger, peeled and thinly
  sliced

3 cups granulated sugar

3 cups water

5 teaspoons tartaric acid

1. Add the lemon slices, honey, ginger, sugar, and measured water to a saucepan, bring to a boil, and then simmer over low heat for about 20 minutes, stirring occasionally, until the sugar has dissolved and the lemons are almost translucent. Remove from the heat and stir in the tartaric acid. Leave to cool.

2. Remove some of the lemon slices using a slotted spoon and set aside. Strain the cordial into sterilized, wide-necked bottles or storage jars and add the reserved lemon slices. Seal well and store in the refrigerator for up to one month.

Elanor and Lissuin Iced Tea

The majority of the flora and fauna that Tolkien describes as flourishing in Middle-earth derive from real-world species. As we traipse around woodlands and fields with the Hobbits in the Shire, as Tolkien describes the stands of oak and beech or the tangled masses of nettles, cow-parsley, and brambles, we may well feel ourselves very much at home. The author was a fine nature writer.

For the landscapes of the Elves, Tolkien occasionally introduced invented, or half-invented, species. Notably in Lothlórien we find the mallorn—massive, beechlike trees that shed their golden fall leaves only in spring, to make way for the new growth. Likewise in Lothlórien, we find the gold-and-silver star-shaped flower elanor, which Tolkien compared to a slightly oversized pimpernel. Another flower beloved of the Elves was the fragrant lissuin, which originally grew on Tol Eressëa (see page 45).

For this cool, refreshing drink we have brought together elanor and lissuin to make a concoction strangely reminiscent of the old British recipe dandelion and burdock. Laze away an afternoon sipping this, on a hammock suspended between mallorn trees.

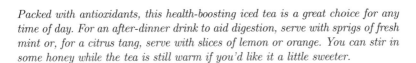

Packed with antioxidants, this health-boosting iced tea is a great choice for any time of day. For an after-dinner drink to aid digestion, serve with sprigs of fresh mint or, for a citrus tang, serve with slices of lemon or orange. You can stir in some honey while the tea is still warm if you'd like it a little sweeter.

Makes 1½ pints
Prep + cook time 15 minutes
  plus steeping

1 tablespoon dried dandelion root
1 tablespoon dried burdock root
3 cups water
ice cubes

1. Put the dandelion and burdock root and the measured water in a saucepan over medium heat and bring to a boil. Turn down the heat and simmer the tea for 10 minutes. Take off the heat and let cool.

2. Strain the tea into a jug or clean bottle. To serve, pour over ice cubes in a tall glass. The tea can be stored in the refrigerator for up to a week.

Goldberry's Nettle Tisane

Tolkien describes nettles, along with hemlock, thistles, and wood-parsley, growing rampantly in the Bonfire Glade of the Old Forest—the clearing where the Brandybuck Hobbit clan once cut down and burned hundreds of trees in a counterattack against the forest after it assailed the High Hay, the dense hedge grown to protect Buckland. Frodo and his companions have now left the Shire and it is the beginning of the fall, and the author paints a rather dismal picture of the clearing in which these wasteland weeds have grown unchecked and are now going to seed.

There's no doubt, though, that Tom Bombadil and his wife, Goldberry—whom the Hobbits are about to meet and who are practiced foragers, it seems, if their meals are anything to go by—make good use of the nettle, which makes a good soup or, as here, a soothing, fresh-tasting tisane.

The nature of Goldberry, the "River-woman's daughter," is much debated—is she a Maia (a lesser spirit and servant of the Valar) or is she something altogether different, a personification of fruitful nature, as Tolkien seems to hint? Whatever her origins, garbed in silver-green and flowerlike, she has the appearance of the Elven queens who abound in European mythologies as well as in Tolkien's legendarium.

Wear rubber gloves to gather the nettle leaves you need for this refreshing tisane. Look for older nettle leaves, as these will taste slightly sweeter (older nettle leaves tend to be longer and less heart-shaped than younger ones). Wash the nettles thoroughly before using them.

Serves 4
Prep + cook time 20 minutes

1 cup nettle leaves, roughly chopped
3 cups water
1 tablespoon sugar or honey, plus extra
   to taste (optional)

1. Put the nettles in a large saucepan with the measured water and sugar or honey, bring to a boil, and leave to simmer for about 15 minutes.

2. Strain and pour into mugs, adding more sugar or honey to taste, if desired.

Lórien's Camomile Tisane

In Tolkien's legendarium, Lórien is a vast garden with abundance of willows, flowers, fountains, and lakes in Valinor—home of the Valar Irmo, Master of Dreams, and his wife Estë, the Healer. It is an Eden and Avalon all in one—both an earthly paradise and a place of rest and healing, suspended between wakefulness and sleep, reality and dream. The Elves of Valinor seek peace and rest there. Gandalf—in his "youth" known as Olórin, as we learn in *The Lord of the Rings*—lived in Lórien for a time; his former name, appropriately, is related to the Quenya word for "dream."

We might imagine Olórin/Gandalf making this relaxing tisane from camomile flowers and handing it to the Elves on their arrival. Weary they may be from their troubles and sorrows but, after drinking this, peace of mind slowly envelops them.

You'll need a juicer to make this nutrient-packed recipe. Fennel contains, among others, vitamins A, C, and B6, as well as iron, calcium, and magnesium, and its aromatic licorice flavor is perfectly complemented by the camomile tea. If you prefer a milder flavor, replace half the fennel with lettuce leaves.

Makes about 7 fl. oz.
Prep time 5 minutes

1 lemon, plus extra to decorate
5 oz. fennel bulb
⅓ cup chilled camomile tea
ice cubes

1. Roughly peel the lemon and juice it with the fennel. Mix the juice with the chilled camomile tea.

2. Pour the combined juice and tea into a glass over ice, and serve with slices of lemon to decorate.

Eöl's Sloe Gin

We know that blackthorn grows in the Shire—Bilbo has composed a walking song mentioning its sharp, ink-black fruits (sloes) that Frodo, Pippin, and Sam sing as they make their way under the trees at Woody End. No doubt the trees grew widely throughout Middle-earth and probably in Beleriand too, so we can imagine that the Elves gathered the fruits as well and put them to good use.

We have named our sloe gin for Eöl, who ruled the small, sunless woodland kingdom of Nan Elmoth, a few leagues east of his kinsman Thingol's realm, Doriath (see page 46). The Elves are complex beings, rarely portrayed as entirely good, but Eöl's temperament is far darker than his peers and his associations are always with blackness and darkness. He has dark eyes (most Elves have gray or blue eyes), is unusually friendly with the Dwarves, a people of the underground, and, himself a master swordsmith, is the inventor of a hard, jet-black metal known as galvorn.

This is a drink that Eöl might have sipped after a long night at his forge, nursing his bitterness and silently plotting revenge.

⌐—••—⌐

Tart but full of rich body and fruity flavor, sloe gin is the ideal winter warmer drunk neat, preferably in front of a roaring fire. To enjoy on a summer evening in the garden, top it with soda or tonic water or, for a special aperitif, with prosecco.

Makes 26 fl. oz.
Prep time 15 minutes, plus storage

5 cups sloe berries
2 cups superfine sugar
2 cups gin

1. Rinse and remove and stems on the sloes and pat them dry with a paper towel. Using a cocktail stick, prick the sloes and place them in a sterilized glass jar large enough to hold the gin.

2. Add the sugar and the gin to the jar and make sure it is securely sealed before giving the jar a good shake. Over the next week, make sure to shake the jar well once a day. Then store the jar in a cool, dark place and leave for two or three months.

3. Strain the gin through a sieve lined with cheesecloth into a bowl, then pour it into a sterilized bottle.

A Laiquendi Cocktail

Of all Tolkien's kindreds of Elves the Laiquendi—the Green-elves—perhaps come closest to the conception of elves found in English folklore: secretive woodland spirits who dress in green and who are famed for their singing. In Tolkien's tales, the Laiquendi are a group of Telerin Elves who settle in the woodlands of Ossiriand, the Land of the Seven Rivers, and who largely keep themselves apart from the rest of the Elves of Beleriand. They are masters of woodlore, use stout wooden bows to hunt and fight, and know the usages of the hundreds of herbs and flowers that grow in their lands.

Perhaps the Laiquendi distilled something like the French liqueur Chartreuse—made with "130 herbs, plants and flowers." Certainly, they would have loved its intense color—green as the leaves of a summer-crowned oak tree.

Naturally a bright green color from all the plants it contains, Green Chartreuse has a sweet, spicy, herby flavor. Its sweetness makes it the perfect foil for gin and, mixed here with vermouth, it creates a very grown-up cocktail.

Serves 1
Prep time 5 minutes

1½ measures gin
1 measure sweet vermouth
½ measure Green Chartreuse
1 dash orange bitters
ice cubes, to serve
cocktail cherry, to decorate

1. Add all of the ingredients to a cocktail shaker or mixing glass, and fill with ice cubes. Stir for 30 seconds, and strain into a chilled martini glass. Decorate with a cocktail cherry.

The Elvenking's Red Wine Punch

In *The Hobbit* the Elvenking's and the Wood-elves' partiality for red wine is an important plot point—not only does the wine make the king's guards drowsy enough for Bilbo to steal the prison keys and free his companions from their prison but the barrels that are used to transport the wine from Lake-town up the Forest River to the Elvenking's halls become the means for Bilbo and the Dwarves to smuggle themselves out of the Elvish kingdom.

The rich, heady red wines most often enjoyed at the Elvenking's tables come from Dorwinion, a land on the northwestern shores of the Sea of Rhûn, far to the east of Mirkwood. For the Elvenking's punch here—perfect for an al fresco lunch in a forest glade—we recommend a rather lighter wine.

Celebrate balmy summer days with this punch. It's fruity, light, and delicious, quick to prep and perfect when entertaining a crowd. You can vary the fruit you include depending on what's in season, but opt for ones that won't disintegrate while sitting in the jug.

Serves 10
Prep time 5 minutes, plus chilling

20–30 ice cubes
2 x 1¼-pint bottles light Spanish red wine, chilled
½ cup brandy (optional)
1½ cups soda water, chilled
slices of fruit such as apples, pears, oranges, lemons, peaches, and strawberries
slices of orange, to decorate

1. Put the ice in a large serving jug, and pour over the wine and brandy, if using. Give everything a stir.

2. Add the soda water and the slices of fruit. If you are making it ahead, add the soda water at the last minute.

3. To serve, decorate the side of each glass with an orange slice and pour in the punch.

Index

Picture Acknowledgments

Victor Ambrus: 3, 7, 14, 21, 25, 42, 58, 79, 89, 96, 111, 114, 124, 128, 155; **Allan Curless:** 139; **Michael Foreman:** endpapers; **Octopus Publishing Group:** Stephen Conroy 30, 33, 91, 127, 136, 156; Will Heap 37, 47, 133, 141; Lis Parsons back cover middle and bottom, 49, 63, 65, 98, 107, 153; William Reavell 57; Craig Roberts 95; William Shaw back cover top, 17, 22, 27, 54, 75, 81, 87, 113; Ian Wallace 105, 117; **iStock** (used throughout): Alhontess, Andrea_Hill, ant_art, bombuscreative, ilbusca, Jon Wightman, Kseniia Gorova, Nastasic, Neil Hubert, Neuevector, smartboy10; **Shutterstock:** NosorogUA spine and front cover.